A PASSION FOR PORK

pig

DUNCAN BAIRD PUBLISHERS

LONDON

A PASSION FOR PORK

pig

Johnnie Mountain

Pig
Johnnie Mountain

Distributed in the USA and Canada by
Sterling Publishing Co., Inc.
387 Park Avenue South
New York, NY 10016-8810

First published in the UK and USA in 2012 by
Duncan Baird Publishers Ltd
Sixth Floor, Castle House, 75–76 Wells Street
London W1T 3QH

Managing Editor: Grace Cheetham
Editor: Nicola Graimes
Americanizer: Beverly LeBlanc
Recipe Tester: Caroline Brewester
Art Direction and Designer: Manisha Patel
Production: Uzma Taj
Commissioned Photography: Yuki Sugiura
Food Stylist: Johnnie Mountain with Aya Nishimura
Prop Stylist: Cynthia Inions
Videography: Yuki Sugiura and Film Infinity

Library of Congress Cataloging-in-Publication
Data available

ISBN: 978-1-84899-039-5

10 9 8 7 6 5 4 3 2 1

Typeset in Nexus Mix
Colour reproduction by XY Digital
Printed in China by Imago

For information about custom editions, special
sales, premium and corporate purchases, please
contact Sterling Special Sales Department at
800-805-5489 or specialsales@sterlingpub.com.

PUBLISHER'S NOTE
While every care has been taken in compiling the
recipes for this book, Duncan Baird Publishers, or any
other persons who have been involved in working on
this publication, cannot accept responsibility for any
errors or omissions, inadvertent or not, that may be
found in the recipes or text, nor for any problems that
may arise as a result of preparing one of these recipes.
It is important that you consult a medical professional
before following any of the recipes or information
contained in this book if you have any special dietary
requirements or medical conditions. Ill or elderly
people, babies, young children and women who are
pregnant or breastfeeding should avoid recipes
containing raw meat or uncooked eggs.

NOTES ON THE RECIPES
Unless otherwise stated:
• All recipes serve 4
• Use large eggs
• Use medium fruit and vegetables
• Use fresh ingredients, including herbs and chilies
• 1 tsp. = 5ml   1 tbsp. = 15ml   1 cup = 240ml

CONTENTS

INTRODUCTION

My greatest childhood memory is definitely my Nana Olga's bacon sandwich; running to her house after school, mouth watering in anticipation of the hand-cut, smoky, crisp bacon sandwiched between two slices of soft, wholewheat, doorstep-thick bread with lashings of melting butter. My love of pork has since grown from a passion to an obsession!

Over the twenty-plus years I've worked as a chef in kitchens across the globe, I've always felt pork has been given the "cheap seat" on menus, and maybe hasn't been treated with the same respect as other types of meat. I wanted to change this, so I opened a restaurant in the heart of the City of London and called it *The English Pig*. For me, pork has so much to offer and now's the time to show the pig in all its glory.

Pork is now often called "the other white meat" as breeders produce leaner and healthier cuts, but the most fantastic thing about pork is its versatility—it provides lean cuts, fattier cuts and cuts for roasting, stewing or braising. Cured, smoked and air-dried pork has become a culinary art in its own right, and has led to some of the most sought-after delicacies in the world, such as Iberico, Serrano, Parma and Bellota hams, as well as spectacular sausages and salami. Pound for pound, the pig is amazing!

With today's modern approach to pig farming, unfortunately there are still varying standards of animal welfare. Although I'm always pleased to discover that there are still a number of amazing farmers who believe in their product, and finding them is of utmost importance to me. I visit farms at least half a dozen times a year, checking on quality control and whether these wonderful omnivores are being looked after in the correct way.

I take sourcing very seriously, and my preference is for outdoor-reared pork, because this allows the hog to follow its natural instincts of foraging and burrowing for its own food. A natural and varied diet is crucial to the flavor of pork, and the pig needs to eat almost constantly. This explains its quick growth: at about nine months old a pig has reached its optimum meat-to-bone ratio. Outdoor rearing allows for socializing and this is a very important trait when making sure the animal is happy within its environment and itself. A calm pig is a happy pig, and a happy pig produces the most amazing meat!

BREEDS OF PIG

There are hundreds, if not thousands, of breeds of pig across the globe, with some breeds reared for their fresh meat and others more suited to cured ham.

Of the fourteen rare breeds I love to cook with, my favorite is the Gloucester Old Spot [1], because the beautiful layers of fat on the belly make it the perfect piece for slow cooking. I also look for British Saddlebacks [2], which are longer in the body, resulting in stunning loins and tenderloins. Sandy and Black, Tamworth and British Lop [3] are also excellent for cooking with due to their great flavor and lean meat content.

In certain parts of Europe, particularly in hilly regions, certain breeds have been chosen for their suitability for ham. All that hill climbing (and acorn eating) gives a wonderful texture and taste to the haunch of the pig. The much-coveted and DOC-protected (Designation of Origin) dry-cured Spanish hams—Iberico, Bellota and jamon Serrano—are some of the most revered. Iberico Black pigs [4] are pure or cross bred with other breeds and mainly come from southern Spain. Bellota ham is from free-range pigs that roam the Iberian peninsula, and whose diet is made up almost entirely of acorns, while Serrano comes mainly from Landrace pigs, but also from Duroc [5] and Pietrain.

Italian Parma and San Daniele are also popular, fine-quality hams and they usually come from the Large White, Landrace or Duroc pigs. The Tuscan equivalent is the La Cinta Senese or Sienese Banded pig, which is much sought after for prosciutto.

Across Eastern and Central Europe, one of the most popular breeds is the Krskopolje, or Blackbelted Pig, which is celebrated for its large size and quality of meat. The Mangalitsa [6] is very popular in Hungary, especially as it has a great fat content with beautiful marbling, making it fantastic for hams and salami. In Germany, the Swabian-Hall is a rare breed that is revered for its fattier flesh and has a geographical status protected by the European Union.

North American breeds are relatively new and mainly bred for their lean meat. The Duroc is probably the most "traditional" and was bred initially in the states of New York and New Jersey in the 1800s. The breed is unique due to its bright auburn skin.

COOKING WITH PORK

Our mothers were most likely taught to cook pork thoroughly, which often made it very dry, but now, due to new standards in pig farming, better guidelines on feed and improvements in transport, you really can eat pork slightly pink! Even the United States Department of Agriculture has fully embraced this trend. In 2011, for example, it reduced the recommended internal temperature for cooked pork from 165°F (thoroughly cooked and possibly dry) to 145°F, where it is slightly rosy and still moist.

When cooking pork, certain cuts suit some dishes better than others. Broadly speaking, the parts of a pig that do a lot of work, such as the legs and jowls, are muscular and tougher, so they need long, slow cooking. Those that do little, such as the tenderloin and loin, are lean and benefit from quick cooking. To make things easy, my suggestions for using each cut of pork will help you to cook this wonderful meat perfectly.

Cooking with pork loin

The loin of a pig is one of the most versatile cuts of pork and it is also one of the most expensive. As with other animals, the muscles in the loin area do very little work, so the meat tends to be lean, and it also has a more subtle flavor than meat from the shoulder or the legs.

A loin roast is one of the most popular roasting cuts and although the meat is fairly lean, it has a good outer layer of fat and skin, which keeps the meat moist and makes fantastic crisp cracklings. Conventional roasting at a higher temperature is ideal for pork loin, although it can also be cooked more gently, if required (see Pork Loin in a Salt & Fennel Crust, page 172). A boneless loin roast is easy to carve and can also be opened out and filled with a stuffing for extra flavor and moisture (see Rolled Loin of Pork with Ricotta & Basil, page 70). Meat roasted on the bone is usually seen as the ultimate way to impart flavor, and a loin rack roast is very manageable for home cooks. If you are concerned about carving, ask a butcher to cut the meat away from the bones, then tie it back on. The meat can then be easily lifted away from the bones for carving after roasting.

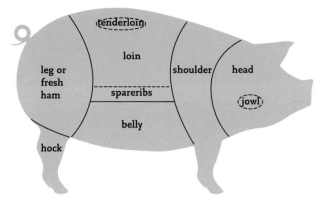

The tenderloin comes from within the loin area and it is very lean and tender [*pictured overleaf, left*]. It is a long, thin cyclindrical cut, 2½ to 3½ inches in diameter with very little fat, although the tenderloin does have a covering of pale white, silvery membrane. This is called the silverskin, a type of connective tissue that doesn't break down when cooked. It can be tough, so it is best removed with a sharp knife before cooking. (See "Show Me How" To Prepare and Cook the Tenderloin, page 68.) The lean tenderloin is best cooked quickly and left slightly pink in the middle so it stays moist and juicy. The shape of the tenderloin makes it ideal for cutting into thin slices or thicker medallions and pan frying (see Pork Medallions with Brandy-Soaked Prunes, page 67). The tenderloin takes strong flavors well, and is particularly good marinated before cooking (see Korean-Style Fiery Pork, page 130). It can also be wrapped in bacon and roasted briefly (see Bacon-Wrapped Tenderloin with Mushroom Stuffing, page 110) or pan-fried whole (see Coriander-Crusted Pork, page 132).

Pork loin chops are great for quick-and-easy weeknight meals. Bone-in chops have both bone and fat to help provide flavor and moisture, and can be quickly pan-fried or broiled (see Broiled Garlic & Sage Pork Chops, page 53). Boneless loin chops can come with or without fat and are fantastic for beating into thin scallops for super-quick cooking (see Pork Saltimbocca, page 109), or cut into pieces or strips for stir-frying (see Sweet & Sour Pork, page 59).

Baby back ribs also come from the loin area of pork. These ribs are always best done in a whole rack, barbecue-style, low and slow (see Sticky Barbecue Ribs, page 168).

Cooking with pork leg

Pork legs from the hindquarters of the pig (either sold fresh or as ham) are heavily muscled and consequently much leaner than the shoulder and belly. Sadly, this part of the pig has probably contributed most to the belief that pork can be dry, because it needs more careful cooking than some other cuts. Maybe, then, it is no surprise that legs are most commonly cured as ham.

Legs can be sold bone-in or boneless, but due to the size of the joint it is usually available boneless and cut into portions. If it is on the bone, try to choose a piece from the lower, or shank, end of the leg as it is a more manageable size and easier to carve.

Pot-roasting is one of the best ways to cook pork leg (see Pot-Roasted Leg of Pork with Sweet Garlic, page 193). This method creates a slightly steamy environment to keep the meat moist during cooking. The leg can also be marinated overnight in oil and herbs for extra flavor. Pork leg comes into its own in slow-cooked curries and stews (see Pork Goulash, page 194), because even after long cooking the meat tends to hold together.

The leg can also be conventionally roasted, but its lower fat content means that it is not the best cut for slow roasting. If you want to roast a leg and keep it moist, then "lard" the meat by threading strips of fatback through the joint, using a special needle called a larding needle, which you can get from good kitchen supply stores or online.

Alternatively, if it is a boneless rolled roast, you can unroll it, stuff it, reroll it and tie it with string. Weigh the stuffed meat and calculate the cooking time at 45 minutes per 2¼ pounds or 20 minutes per pound, plus an extra 30 minutes. Preheat the oven to 425°F and roast the leg 30 minutes to crisp the skin, then reduce the temperature to 350°F for the remaining time. Like most meat, a roasted leg needs to rest after cooking.

Leg steaks can be dry, so they should be marinated and then cooked very quickly and left a little pink. Because the muscle fibers in the leg are very long, it can be useful to tenderize the meat before cooking by beating it with a meat mallet or rolling pin. The meat can also be cut across the grain into thin strips to use for stir-frying.

Cooked ham can be bought bone-in or boneless, and again for most home cooks a boneless ham is a more manageable option. It can be smoked or unsmoked, and since most ham today tends to be mild-cured, it will probably not need soaking before cooking. If you are not sure about its saltiness, however, test it first by following my tip on Homecooked Ham in Ginger & Mustard Glaze (see page 210). Uncooked ham should be rinsed and soaked according to the supplier's directions before cooking. It is best simmered in water rather than roasted, because this is a more gentle form of cooking. You can roast a larger bone-in ham, however, if first soaked overnight, drained, then wrapped in foil. Preheat the oven to 325°F and roast 45 minutes per 2¼ pounds or 20 minutes per pound, followed by glazing and baking at a higher temperature for a glossy coating.

Cooking with pork shoulder

If you look at a pork roast from the shoulder, you are likely to notice there is a fair amount of fat marbling through the meat or muscle, which makes it very flavorful and also ideal for slow cooking, because the meat remains moist while the fat melts away. The structure of the meat also means that it tends to fall apart once it has been cooked.

The shoulder covers a large area of the pig, and it is commonly sold as Boston butt and picnic shoulder, which comes from the lower part of the shoulder. Meat from the shoulder is sold both bone-in and boneless.

Shoulder roasts with their skin on are perfect for slow roasting (see Eight-Hour Roasted Shoulder of Pork, page 170). Make sure you score the skin first so it crisps as the fat renders away, producing delicious cracklings. You need a blast of high heat, preferably at the beginning of roasting, for successful cracklings. The high heat will also help to color the outside of the meat and leave caramelized bits (called the *fond*) on the bottom and sides of the roasting tin, which you can then use to make flavorsome gravy.

Shoulder cuts are also good for barbecuing very slowly over wood chips. Again, the fat content helps keep the meat moist and the cooked pork is easy to shred or pull apart, making it the cut of choice for southern pulled pork.

Pork steaks, or blade steaks, also come from the shoulder. The meat from this cut can be on the tough side, so blade steaks should be cooked very quickly and left slightly pink. Pan-frying is the best method for cooking shoulder steaks; make sure the pan is very hot before you add the meat, which can be flavored with a rub of herby or spicy salt before cooking. If the shoulder is cubed and stewed, then it tends to break down into shreds, making it perfect for ragus or other meat-based sauces.

The very bottom part of the shoulder, extending down to the leg, is known as the knuckle, or pork tip; this is the "elbow" section before you reach the feet. Ham or pork hocks come from the lower part of the shank and can be cured or uncured. Either way, however, they need very long, slow cooking until the meat literally falls away from the bone. A ham hock is best covered in liquid and simmered, because the curing process can leave the meat a little dry if it is braised or roasted, although like other hams it can be finished in the oven. The best way to cook an uncured knuckle is to braise it in a little liquid to keep it moist, then finish with a period of high heat to crisp the skin on the outside (see Braised Pork Knuckle in Cider, page 206).

Cooking with pork belly

If there was ever a piece of meat that has gone from cheap cut to culinary superstar then it has to be pork belly. The fatty underside of the pig used to be routinely overlooked by

loin

tenderloin

belly

ribs

loin

pork chop

belly and
middle cut

ribs

home cooks, but in more recent years its true value has been recognized. When cooked, the layers of skin, flesh and fat give an optimal mix of crisp, crackling shards of skin and flavorsome tender meat. The belly has now been firmly embraced by cooks in the West, but it shouldn't come as a surprise to learn Asians have revered this cut for some time. Not only does pork belly taste great, it's also versatile: it can be preserved (see Confit of Pork Belly, page 181, and How to Cure Bacon, page 98); braised (see Japanese Pork Belly, page 192) or roasted (see Slow-Roasted Pork Belly, page 189).

Pork belly is made up of a layer of skin, a subcutaneous layer of fat, a layer of muscle, a second layer of fat plus connective tissue and a second layer of muscle. This lamination of fat and meat gives the belly its fantastic flavor and also plenty of moisture, which means slow roasting is perhaps the best way of all to cook it. An initial blast of high heat in the oven will start to blister and crisp the scored skin, but after this the oven needs to be turned down to low to let the fat slowly melt away. Pork belly needs very little attention during roasting. To prevent the pork sitting in a pool of grease while it roasts, however, it's best to sit the belly on a "trivet" of chopped vegetables, or on a metal rack, so the rendered fat slides away into the bottom of the pan.

Because the belly retains lots of moisture during cooking, it is an ideal cut to cook ahead. First braise the belly in an aromatic stock, then let cool and chill until ready to serve. Before serving, portion the meat and reheat it fairly quickly in a hot pan or oven—this is one restaurant trick that works well in a home kitchen. The gelatin from the meat enriches the braising liquid and it can then be reduced down to make a delicious accompanying sauce or gravy, once the fat has been skimmed away (see Chinese Pork Belly with Seasoned Rice, page 186).

One of the ways I like to cook pork belly in my restaurants is to braise it 16 hours with carrots and onions until it is so tender the meat literally falls apart. The pork is then shredded, keeping the paler upper and darker lower layers separate, and pressed in alternate layers with the braised vegetables. Finally, it is cut into squares, bread-crumbed, fried and cut into wedges for serving. It is the ultimate pork "sandwich!"

Cooking with the rest of the pig

There is a popular saying about the pig that "you can eat everything but the squeal." In recent years there has been a revival in the popularity of nose-to-tail eating, and cuts like feet appear on more restaurant menus and even in more supermarkets.

There are many classic dishes that celebrate the feet, such as *crubeens* from Ireland, *pied de cochon* from France and the spicy Korean *jokbal*. Pickled pigs' feet are also popular in many cuisines. The one thing that these recipes all have in common, however, is the initial long, slow cooking. One of the wonderful by-products of this technique is that you will end up with a stock rich in gelatin, ideal for savory pies and terrines. The remaining feet can then be cooked in many ways: stuffed, baked, coated in bread crumbs or cooked in a rich sauce and served in slices. As an added benefit, some people believe eating the collagen in the feet keeps you looking young!

A pig's head is also very versatile, but often ends up as a terrine called, rather unglamorously, head cheese, or brawn. The head is usually soaked in brine first, then slowly poached in a spiced stock until the meat can be pulled away from the bones and shredded. Often feet are added to increase the meat content and for a richer stock. The meat is then packed into a terrine or bowl and covered with the strained stock, which forms a gel when chilled. Head cheese is served sliced, usually with toast and a salad.

A hog's jowl, however, is by far and away the hidden treasure. All animal jowls do a lot of work and are, therefore, fairly tough, but when cooked slowly they become amazingly tender and, again, the collagen in the meat oozes out to deliver an incredibly rich sauce. As a hog's jowl is fairly small, you will need two per person, but the size is also an advantage because it means it cooks more quickly than some of the larger cuts. If you were going to try any of the more unusual cuts of pork, I urge you to try this one (see Hog Jowls with Caramelized Fennel, page 204).

While it is true that you can't make a silk purse out of a sow's ear, you can turn this part of the pig into a tasty treat. The ear is mainly fat and cartilage and is really best cooked until crisp (see Crisp Pig Ears, page 165). The crisp morsels can be served as a snack or appetizer, or even as a crunchy garnish to a salad. A word of warning, however: the ear retains a lot of liquid so it tends to spit when it hits the hot fat.

Now to the tail... although perceived as a skinny part of the anatomy, the tail does contain some meat and a good amount of fat. It is particularly popular in the Caribbean and some of the southern states. It can be stewed, but is most popular braised until tender, then roasted or barbecued until crisp.

PRESERVED PORK

Most popular methods of pork preservation have been around for thousands of years. Pigs were traditionally slaughtered in the late fall, partly because it was expensive and impractical to feed animals during the winter and partly because they would have been fattened during the warmer months on windfalls, nuts and seeds. Charcuterie, which comes from the French words *chair*, meaning "flesh," and *cuite*, meaning "cooked," was developed to improve the keeping qualities of meat during the cooler winter months.

Pretty much all pork preservation starts with curing: treating the meat with salt, either mixed with water to make a brine, or by applying a dry salt mixture to the surface of the meat. The salt draws out moisture from the meat, which is vital for preservation because bacteria needs moisture to grow. Salt also slows down the fermentation process that breaks down the meat fibers, keeping the meat firm. Alongside salt, saltpeter and, more recently, sodium nitrate or nitrite, is added to help stop the meat deteriorating and to prevent bacteria formation.

Bacon and ham are probably the most popular types of preserved pork. They are made in a similar manner with ham cured for longer than bacon (see How to Cure Bacon, page 98). In many countries, ham is air-dried after curing and matured to preserve it even more and enhance its flavor, such as prosciutto, Iberico and jamon Serrano. Prosciutto ham takes between nine months and two years before it is ready to be eaten. Ham and bacon can also be smoked for additional flavor, although smoking in itself does not preserve pork. Ham and bacon are usually hung in a smokehouse and cold smoked for up to two days. Pork can also be almost completely dried to make jerky, which is popular in South Africa.

Salame, or *saucisson sec*, is a sausage that is cured and air dried to preserve it. Usually a mixture of pork shoulder and fat is finely chopped or ground and mixed with a curing salt mixture before being stuffed into a sausage casing. Salame differs from ham in that it is fermented first, often by adding acidophilus, a type of "friendly" bacteria. It is perfectly safe to eat and often seen as the dry white bloom on the outside of an artisanal salame. The salame is then air-dried for several weeks and often a white mold is applied to the casing to reduce exposure to air and improve its keeping qualities. It is possible to make salame at home, although it is advisable to test its pH balance after the initial fermentation to make sure it is safe to eat. You will also need to have a cool place with good air circulation for drying the salame.

Preserving in fat is also a popular way to keep pork (see Goose Fat Potted Pork, page 76). French rillettes, for example, is one of the earliest types of pâté and is made by slowly cooking pork in pork fat until very tender. The meat is then shredded, packed into sterilized jars and covered with the fat. Confit pork is similar, although cooked in goose or duck fat, rather than pork fat, and the meat is usually left in larger pieces (see Confit of Pork Belly, page 181).

CHOOSING PORK

Good meat comes from good farming. A happy pig is more likely to give soft, succulent flesh than one that has been raised in a stressful environment. Flavor is also influenced by a hog's diet, with a natural and varied diet more likely to give tastier meat than a bland, monotonous one. While rearing standards have improved enormously over the years, in some places they are still not perfect, so it is very important to try and buy from stores that know the source or provenance of their meat. A local butcher is usually the ideal place to shop, but this is not always an option for many people. Some supermarket chains, however, only buy from reliable sources and can trace the origins of their pork, and it is worth supporting those that assure high welfare standards. Packaging can be misleading, but look for stores selling outdoor-reared pork. It's better to buy a smaller amount of good-quality pork than a huge cut of inferior meat—your taste buds will thank you for this.

When buying fresh pork it should be dry, not sitting in a pool of liquid. Read the label to make sure the meat does not have any added water. Also, although this is rare, it is worth checking the packaging to make sure that there are not unwanted additives. The flesh should look plump and firm, not limp and flabby, and there should not be any signs of discoloration or a "rainbow" sheen, which means that the pork is not at its best. When you touch the pork, it shouldn't feel sticky, because this means bacteria has started to form on the outer skin, neither should it feel slimy. There should also not be any odor.

If you are buying cured meat, again the quality affects the price you pay. If you are splashing out on a premium air-dried ham, make sure that it is from a reputable supplier and it has the DOC, or other appropriate origin stamps. Buying dry-cured bacon is worth the extra money for its superior flavor and great texture.

STORING PORK

When you get fresh pork home, store it on the bottom shelf of the refrigerator. If the meat is wrapped in plastic, remove the wrapping, then transfer the meat to a dish and cover loosely with foil or plastic wrap. This helps air flow around the meat and prevents it from sweating; it should then be good for about 2 days. If you want to freeze the pork, wrap it tightly in fresh plastic wrap and put the meat in a resealable bag, expelling as much air as possible. It can then be frozen up to 3 months, and always defost pork thoroughly in the refrigerator before cooking.

Cured meats should be well wrapped, because they can dehydrate quickly in the dry air of the refrigerator. Packaged hams and salami come with a best-if-used-by date, and they can be frozen up to three months, if required. If freezing bacon, you might like to wrap the slices in single-portion quantities, ready to be defrosted quickly and easily whenever they are required.

ABOUT THIS BOOK

Pork is often seen as the best example of nose-to-tail eating and it's easy to see why in this book. The sheer versatility of pork compared to other meats has to be admired, especially in the way it adapts to both different styles of cooking and to different flavors. My signature dish (see Slow-Roasted Pork Belly, page 189) at my London restaurant, *The English Pig*, is constantly evolving with new modern versions of a great traditional ingredient. I have also been known to create a ten-course "pigfest"—a true celebration of the pig!

I hope I give you a taste of this celebration in my book, because within these pages you'll find a wide selection of recipes to suit all types of meal and eating occasion. I've included family favorites and everyday suppers, slow-cooked meals and even a few show-stopping dinner-party centerpieces. There are also recipes that make the most of bacon, ham and other cured meats, as well as sizzling spicy dishes from around the world.

On a more practical note, I've given you lots of tips on the best ways to cook specific cuts, and there's also informative advice in the "How To..." features within each chapter. These take you through a selection of simple techniques, such as braising, making sausages, home smoking, curing your own bacon and, not forgetting, roasting the best pork loin with perfect, crisp cracklings! You'll notice that some pages also have a QR code that will link you to a video clip showing a useful technique, helping you to pick up a few restaurant tricks of the trade along the way.

My experience of cooking in restaurants around the world, as well as the many adventures at my own restaurants, have shown me how much can be done with this fabulous creature and now I want to share these recipes with you, too.

CHAPTER 1

HOME FAVORITES

Pork is an incredibly versatile meat and this means there is a cut to suit most tastes, budgets and occasions. You'll find a great mix of recipes in this chapter, from breakfast and lunch to midweek meals and special dinners. There are popular classic dishes from all over the world alongside family favorites, some of which have been adapted to use pork.

If you are looking for something quick, boneless pork loin chops can be cooked in next to no time. Why not try coating thin slices in golden cheesy crumbs like the Pork Scallops in Parmesan Crust, or stir-frying them, as in the Sweet & Sour Pork? Ground pork can be turned into Pork Meatballs and served with linguine for a speedy midweek meal, and Broiled Garlic & Sage Pork Chops make a satisfying family dinner. Good-quality link sausages are also a great standby for busy households. Try Sausages in Spiced Apple Relish or cocooned in a light, crisp batter for the best Toad-in-the-Hole with Onion Gravy.

Pork tenderloin is a great cut if you want to make something slightly more special for the weekend, perhaps Pork Tenderloin with Mustard Sauce or Pork Medallions with Brandy-Soaked Prunes. Or, impress friends and family with my helpful tips and recipe for Roast Pork Loin with its perfect cracklings.

4 slices of country-style sourdough bread,
  or 8 thick slices from a large loaf of ciabatta
2 garlic cloves, cut in half
1 to 2 tablespoons extra virgin olive oil
1 to 2 tablespoons vegetable oil

4 eggs
4 thick slices good-quality baked ham
1 small handful parsley leaves, chopped
  (optional)
salt and freshly ground black pepper

SERVES 4 | **PREPARATION TIME** 5 minutes | **COOKING TIME** 5 minutes

BREAKFAST BRUSCHETTA

This gives a whole new meaning to "breakfast in a flash." Bacon and eggs on toast will never seem the same again!

1] Toast both sides of the bread. If you can do this on a cast-iron ridged grill pan, then all the better. Rub the cut sides of the garlic all over the toast, then brush or drizzle a little olive oil over each slice.

2] Heat the vegetable oil in a large skillet over medium heat. Fry the eggs until cooked as you like them—I prefer the yolks soft and slightly runny. Season with a little salt and pepper.

3] Lay a slice of ham on each piece of toast (or, if using ciabatta, on top of 2 slices), then top with a fried egg. Serve sprinkled with a little parsley, if you like.

2¼ pounds Yukon Gold potatoes, peeled and cut into large chunks

½ head Savoy cabbage, stems removed and leaves thinly sliced

2 tablespoons unsalted butter

2 tablespoons milk or cream

freshly grated nutmeg

12 slices dry-cured smoked bacon

salt and freshly ground black pepper

SERVES 4 | **PREPARATION TIME** 20 minutes | **COOKING TIME** 1 hour

BUBBLE & SQUEAK WITH DRY-CURED BACON

Bubble and squeak was originally a way to use up leftover vegetables. If using leftovers, you will need about 4½ cups cold mashed potatoes and 1½ cups cooked shredded cabbage. It's well worth making this from scratch, however, and you can also top each serving with a fried egg for a delicious brunch.

1] Put the potatoes in a large saucepan of cold salted water over high heat. Bring to a boil, then turn down the heat and cook 15 to 20 minutes until the potatoes are tender. Drain the potatoes and leave them in a strainer or colander 10 minutes to let them cool slightly.

2] Meanwhile, cook the cabbage in a pan of boiling salted water 2 to 3 minutes until just tender, but not soft. Drain and cool the cabbage quickly by rinsing it under cold running water. Leave to drain 10 minutes.

3] Put the potatoes in a large bowl and mash with the butter and milk. Mix in the cabbage and season with salt, pepper and nutmeg.

4] Put the bacon in a large, dry nonstick skillet over low heat. (You might need to cook this dish in two batches, depending on the size of your skillet.) Cook about 10 minutes, turning halfway through, until the fat starts to melt out of the bacon. Turn up the heat to medium and fry the bacon 4 to 5 minutes longer until crisp. Transfer the bacon to a plate lined with paper towels, leaving the bacon fat in the skillet.

5] Add the potato mixture to the skillet, pressing it into a flat disk. Cook over medium-high heat 3 to 4 minutes until a crust forms on the bottom. Using a metal spatula, stir the mixture slightly, so the crust is folded through the potatoes. Press the mixture down again and cook 3 to 4 minutes longer. Repeat this 3 or 4 times so the potatoes are streaked with delicious ribbons of crusted potatoes.

6] Break half of the bacon into pieces and fold through the potatoes, then put the remainder on top. Serve straight from the skillet.

HOME FAVORITES

8 soft wheat tortillas, each about 7 inches
   in diameter
8 thin slices good-quality cooked ham, about
   6 ounces total weight, torn into small strips
1 large sweet apple, such as Pink Lady or Fuji,
   peeled, quartered, cored and thinly sliced
2 fresh red chilies, seeded and finely chopped
2 pinches red pepper flakes, or to taste
1¾ cups shredded Monterey Jack cheese
vegetable oil, for greasing
4 tablespoons sour cream, to serve

GUACAMOLE
1 large avocado, halved, pitted and flesh
   scooped out
1 garlic clove, crushed
2 scallions, finely chopped
juice of 1 lime
salt and freshly ground black pepper

SERVES 4 | **PREPARATION TIME** 15 minutes | **COOKING TIME** 20 minutes

HAM & APPLE QUESADILLAS

**Ham and cheese is a popular combination and when partnered with apple and chilies
in a toasted quesadilla it becomes irresistible. If you can't find Monterey Jack cheese,
try using a combination of half mozzarella and half medium cheddar.**

1] First make the guacamole. Put the avocado in a nonmetallic bowl with the garlic,
scallions and lime juice. Season with salt and pepper, then mash with a fork until mixed
together. Set to one side until ready to serve.

2] Lay 4 of the tortillas on a large cutting board and scatter the ham over the tops. Lay the
apple slices on top of the ham, then scatter the chilies and red pepper flakes to taste
over. Sprinkle with the cheese and top with the remaining tortillas.

3] Heat a large skillet over medium-low heat and grease lightly with a little oil. Slide one
of the quesadillas into the pan and cook 2 minutes until brown on the underside. Using
a large, flexible spatula, carefully turn the quesadilla over and cook 2 to 3 minutes longer
until the cheese melts and the tortilla is crisp. Slide onto a plate and keep warm while
you cook the remaining quesadillas.

4] Leave the quesadillas to stand 3 to 4 minutes, then cut each one into slices. Don't cut
them too quickly after cooking or the cheese will just ooze out. Serve the quesadillas
with the guacamole and sour cream.

5 to 6 thick smoked bacon slices

2 tablespoons maple syrup

4 tablespoons extra virgin olive oil

2 tablespoons good-quality balsamic vinegar

7 ounces baby spinach leaves

1 large nectarine, pitted and thinly sliced

¾ cup pecan halves, roughly broken

1 fresh red chili, seeded and thinly sliced

salt and freshly ground black pepper

crusty bread, to serve

SERVES 4 | **PREPARATION TIME** 15 minutes | **COOKING TIME** 15 minutes

BACON & NECTARINE SALAD

The contrast of the crisp, salty bacon with the sweet maple syrup will make your taste buds dance with delight!

1] Preheat the oven to 400°F. Lay the bacon in a single layer on a wire rack set over a roasting pan, lined with foil. Roast 10 minutes, then brush both sides of the slices with the maple syrup and roast 2 to 3 minutes longer until golden and slightly crisp. Remove the bacon from the oven and leave it to cool 2 minutes, because the maple glaze will be very hot, then break into bite-size pieces.

2] Whisk together the oil and vinegar, then season with salt and pepper. Put the spinach in a large serving bowl and toss with most of the dressing. Add the nectarine and bacon and gently mix in. Scatter the pecans and chili over the top. Drizzle the remaining dressing over the salad and serve immediately with slices of crusty bread.

JOHNNIE'S TIP

Roasting bacon on a rack in the oven is a great way to cook it for large numbers of people. You can also flavor it with other ingredients, such as paprika, honey or even a little apricot jam that has been thinned with a small amount of water to make it more spreadable.

"SHOW ME HOW" TO ROAST THE BACON

10 ounces fingerling potatoes

4 extra-large eggs

7 ounces lardons, cubetti di pancetta or
diced smoked bacon

olive oil, as needed

1 tablespoon red wine vinegar
or sherry vinegar

½ teaspoon sugar, or to taste

1 head frisée lettuce, pale inner leaves
only, torn

freshly ground black pepper

baguette or crusty bread, to serve

SERVES 4 | **PREPARATION TIME** 15 minutes | **COOKING TIME** 35 minutes

EGG, BACON & POTATO SALAD

Runny egg, crisp bacon and bittersweet frisée make a perfect combination.

1] Put the potatoes in a large saucepan of cold salted water over high heat. Bring to a boil, then turn down the heat and cook 12 to 15 minutes until tender. Drain and leave to one side to cool slightly, then break or cut into bite-size slices.

2] Meanwhile, put the eggs in a large saucepan and add enough cold water to cover them by ½ inch. Bring to a boil over high heat, then remove the pan from the heat and leave the eggs to stand 12 minutes. Drain the eggs and cool them under cold running water, giving them a little tap to crack the shells. When the eggs are cool, peel and halve them, then leave to one side.

3] To desalt the lardons, put them in a medium-sized saucepan and just cover with water. Bring the water to simmering point, then drain and repeat this process. Drain again and pat dry with paper towels. Put the lardons in a large, dry skillet over low heat. Cook 8 to 10 minutes, turning occasionally, until the fat seeps out of the lardons, then turn up the heat to medium and fry 3 to 4 minutes longer until golden and crisp. Put a strainer over a measuring jug and tip the lardons into the strainer, letting the fat drip into the jug.

4] Add enough olive oil to the lardon fat to make ¼ cup, then whisk in the vinegar and sugar to make a dressing. Season with pepper (you are unlikely to need salt, because the lardons are very salty), taste and add more sugar if the dressing is too sharp.

5] Mix the potatoes, frisée, lardons and eggs gently together in a bowl and drizzle the dressing over the top. Serve with slices of baguette or crusty bread.

"SHOW ME HOW" TO DESALT THE LARDONS

1½ cups dry split green peas, rinsed

1 smoked ham hock, about 1 pound 10 ounces total weight

2 large onions, 1 quartered and the other finely chopped

2 large carrots, 1 scrubbed and halved and the other finely diced

6 black peppercorns

1 bay leaf

1 stick (½ cup) unsalted butter

1 large leek, finely chopped

2 celery stalks, finely diced

6 cups vegetable stock

1 bouquet garni

salt and freshly ground black pepper

crusty bread, to serve

SERVES 4 | **PREPARATION TIME** 15 minutes, plus overnight soaking | **COOKING TIME** 4 hours

HAM, LEEK & PEA SOUP

Classic pea and ham soup doesn't look that great, but the flavor is amazing. This is an old family recipe passed down through many generations of Mountains!

1] Put the split peas in a large bowl. Cover with cold water and leave to soak overnight.

2] Put the ham hock in a large saucepan and cover with cold water. Add the quartered onion, halved carrot, peppercorns and bay leaf. Bring the water to a boil, then turn down the heat to low and simmer, part-covered, 2 hours. Drain the ham, reserving 1 cup of the cooking liquid and discard the remainder with the cooked vegetables.

3] Meanwhile, drain the split peas, rinse and drain again. Leave to one side.

4] Melt the butter in a second large saucepan over low heat. Add the remaining onion and carrot as well as the leek and celery. Cook about 15 minutes, stirring occasionally, until soft but not colored. Add the drained peas, vegetable stock and bouquet garni. Transfer the ham hock to the pan. Bring the stock to a boil, then turn down the heat and simmer, part-covered, 1 to 1½ hours until the peas start to disintegrate and the ham is coming away from the bone.

5] Remove the ham from the pan and pull away the meat, tearing it into bite-size chunks. Discard any skin, fat and the bone. Remove the bouquet garni and season the soup with salt and pepper, to taste. (You can puree the soup using a hand blender at this stage if you prefer it smooth, adding some of the ham cooking liquid if it is too thick.)

6] Return the ham to the soup, stir and warm gently over low heat before serving with crusty bread.

1¾ cups white bread flour, plus extra
  for dusting

1 envelope (¼-oz.) instant (bread machine)
  yeast

½ teaspoon salt, plus extra to taste

½ teaspoon sugar

3 tablespoons olive oil, plus extra for greasing

1¾ ounces pancetta or thin smoked
  bacon slices

4 large onions, thinly sliced

4 thyme sprigs

15 black olives, pitted and halved

freshly ground black pepper

green salad, to serve

SERVES 4 to 6 | **PREPARATION TIME** 1½ hours, including rising | **COOKING TIME** 30 minutes

PROVENÇAL BACON & ONION TART

The sweet onions are offset by a salty kick in this popular French onion tart, but here the saltiness comes from the pancetta, rather than the usual anchovies.

1] Mix together the flour, yeast, salt and sugar in a large bowl. Make a well in the middle and add 1 tablespoon of the olive oil, plus ½ cup hand-hot water (100° to 110°F). Mix together, adding more water as needed to make a soft dough. Turn out the dough onto a lightly floured work surface and knead about 10 minutes until smooth and springy. Lightly grease a clean bowl with a little olive oil. Put the dough in the bowl, cover with plastic wrap and leave to rise in a warm place 1 hour, or until double in size.

2] Meanwhile, cook the pancetta in a large, dry nonstick skillet over medium heat 6 minutes, turning once, until crisp. Remove the pancetta from the pan, then leave to cool slightly. Break the pancetta into pieces and leave to one side on a plate lined with paper towels.

3] Add the onions to the pan along with the remaining 2 tablespoons olive oil, thyme and 2 tablespoons water. Cover the pan and turn down the heat to low. Cook the onions about 40 minutes, stirring regularly, until very soft. Remove the lid and increase the heat to medium, then cook 5 to 10 minutes longer to remove any excess moisture. Season the onions with salt and pepper, remove the thyme sprigs and leave the onions to one side.

4] Preheat the oven to 400°F. Lightly oil the bottom but not the sides of a large baking tray.

5] Tip the dough into the baking tray and press it out to cover the bottom and up the sides. Spread the onions in an even layer over the dough and top with the olives and pancetta pieces. Bake 25 to 30 minutes until the bottom of the dough is golden and crisp. Leave the tart to cool slightly, then serve with a green salad.

2⅔ cups all-purpose flour, plus extra
    for dusting

½ teaspoon salt

2 eggs, lightly beaten

3 tablespoons unsalted butter

5 tablespoons vegetable shortening

pickle or chutney, to serve

GELATIN

1 ham bone or 7 ounces pork bones

1 onion, quartered

1 carrot, scrubbed and cut into 2-inch pieces

1 celery stalk, cut in half

1 bay leaf

4 black peppercorns

1 gelatin leaf (2g)

FILLING

7 ounces boneless pork shoulder or Boston
    butt, cubed

3 slices bacon, about 1¾ ounces
    total weight

3 large sage leaves, finely chopped

4 dried apricots, finely chopped

⅛ teaspoon ground allspice

freshly grated nutmeg

vegetable oil, for frying and greasing

salt and freshly ground black pepper

MAKES 8 | PREPARATION TIME 2 hours, plus an initial chilling & overnight chilling |
COOKING TIME 45 minutes

PORK PIES [*pictured overleaf*]

True satisfaction is producing your own pork pie! Don't be scared of attempting the hot-water crust, because the pastry dough really is straightforward to make.

1] To make the pastry dough, sift the flour and salt into a large bowl and stir in one of the eggs. Melt the butter, shortening and ⅔ cup cold water over low heat. Turn up the heat to high and bring the mixture to a boil, then immediately remove the pan from the heat and stir the hot fat into the flour, mixing with a wooden spoon until it forms a thick paste. Put the paste on a large piece of plastic wrap and pat into a disk, then wrap and refrigerate 1 hour.

2] Meanwhile, to make the gelatin, put the ham bone, onion, carrot, celery and 4 cups water in a medium-sized saucepan. Bring to a boil, skimming any foamy scum that rises to the surface of the water, then turn down the heat to low. Add the bay leaf and peppercorns and simmer very gently 1 hour.

3] To make the filling, finely chop the pork and bacon by hand or in a food processor (use "pulse" so the meat isn't too finely ground). Put the pork and bacon in a bowl and stir in the sage, apricots, allspice and several gratings of nutmeg. [*continued on page 37*]

Season with salt and pepper. Fry 1 teaspoon of the mixture, then taste, adding more allspice, nutmeg, salt and pepper, if required. The filling will taste milder when cold, so be generous with the seasoning.

4] Preheat the oven to 350°F. Roll out two-thirds of the dough on a lightly floured surface until ⅛ inch thick. Using a 3½-inch-round cutter, press out 8 circles. Lightly grease 8 cups of a muffin pan and put a circle of dough in each. Press the dough into the bottom and up the side of each cup, leaving a slight overhang. Put a heaped tablespoonful of the filling into each dough case.

5] Roll out the remaining dough to ¹⁄₁₆ inch thick and cut out 8 more circles using a 2¾-inch-round cutter. Brush the edges of the pies with some of the remaining beaten egg and put the dough circle tops on, crimping the edges with a small fork to seal. Decorate with the dough trimmings, if you like. Glaze the pies with the remaining beaten egg, then cut a steam hole in the top of each pie (make sure it is fairly open). Bake 30 minutes until the pastry is golden brown. Cool slightly in the pan, then use a table knife to ease out the pies and cool on a wire rack 1 hour.

6] Meanwhile, strain the ham bone cooking liquid into a clean saucepan, discarding the bone and vegetables. Bring to a boil over high heat and boil until the liquid reduces to slightly less than ½ cup, then remove the pan from the heat and season with salt and pepper. Soak the gelatin leaf in cold water 5 minutes until soft and pliable, then squeeze it out and whisk into the hot liquid until it dissolves. Using a pipette or teaspoon, carefully add a little of the liquid into each pie through the steam hole. You should just see the liquid covering the surface of the cooked pork. Leave the pies to cool.

7] Refrigerate the pork pies overnight to let the gelatin set and the flavors develop slightly before serving with a spoonful of relish or chutney.

JOHNNIE'S TIP

To make the gelatin mixture from scratch, without using leaf gelatin, add a pig's foot to the pan with the ham bone or pork bones and pour in enough water to just cover. Bring to a boil, then turn down the heat and simmer 1 hour. Strain the liquid and reduce as in Step 6, above. Let the liquid stand in a cool place 1 hour and skim off as much fat from the surface as possible. Warm gently before pouring it into the pies.

"SHOW ME HOW" TO MOLD AND FILL THE PORK PIES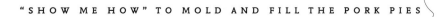

1 thyme sprig, leaves finely chopped

1 oregano sprig, leaves finely chopped

2 fat garlic cloves, finely chopped

3 tablespoons olive oil

1 pound lean boneless pork loin, cut into
24 x ½-inch cubes

2 large lemons, cut into 16 pieces

8 slices smoked bacon, each cut into 3 pieces

24 baby button mushrooms, wiped clean

salt and freshly ground black pepper

boiled white rice and green salad, to serve

SERVES 4 | **PREPARATION TIME** 30 minutes, plus at least 8 hours marinating | **COOKING TIME** 10 minutes

PORK KEBABS

Smoked bacon is the perfect broiling companion to lean meat, while the charred lemons give a zesty lift to these wonderful kebabs.

1] Put the herbs and garlic in a medium bowl and season with a good grinding of black pepper. Stir in the oil, then add the pork and turn to coat the meat in the marinade. Cover and leave to marinate in the refrigerator 8 hours, or overnight.

2] Meanwhile, soak 8 wooden skewers in warm water at least 30 minutes before cooking to prevent them burning.

3] Preheat the broiler to high. Thread a piece of lemon, skin-side down, onto one skewer, pushing it down to almost the end. Thread on a piece of bacon, a cube of pork and a mushroom. Repeat with the bacon, pork and mushrooms twice more, then finish with a piece of lemon, skin-side outward. Repeat to make 8 kebabs in total.

4] Lay the kebabs on the broiler pan and season with a little salt. Brush the kebabs with some of the marinade and broil 8 to 10 minutes, turning regularly, until the mushrooms and pork are brown and the lemons are slightly charred. Put the kebabs fairly close to the heat source so the pork doesn't overcook on the inside as it browns on the outside.

5] Serve the kebabs, squeezing the broiled lemon pieces from the ends of the skewers over the meat and mushrooms, with rice and a green salad.

2 tablespoons vegetable oil

8 good-quality link sausages, about
   1 pound total weight

1 recipe quantity Johnnie's Mashed Potatoes
   (see page 215), to serve

SPICED APPLE RELISH

1/3 cup raisins

1 onion, finely chopped

1/4 teaspoon ground allspice

1/4 teaspoon ground cinnamon

2 apples, such as Pink Lady or Fuji,
   peeled, cored and diced

1 tablespoon apple cider vinegar

2 teaspoons soft light brown sugar,
   plus extra to taste

6 large sage leaves, finely shredded

salt and freshly ground black pepper

SERVES 4 | **PREPARATION TIME** 30 minutes, plus soaking | **COOKING TIME** 40 minutes

SAUSAGES IN SPICED APPLE RELISH [*pictured overleaf*]

Good-quality sausages are a must. Ideally, they should have a slightly coarse texture and contain at least 80 percent pork meat. For the best flavor, look for sausages made by a local butcher or choose the premium ones in your supermarket.

1] To begin the relish, put the raisins in a bowl and cover with just-boiled water. Leave to soak 30 minutes until plumped up, then drain and set to one side.

2] Heat 1 tablespoon of the oil in a large skillet over medium heat. Add the sausages and fry 15 minutes, turning regularly, or until golden brown all over and cooked through. Transfer the sausages to a plate and keep warm.

3] To make the apple relish, add the remaining oil to the skillet and cook the onion, stirring occasionally, 6 to 8 minutes until soft and translucent. Stir in the allspice and cinnamon and cook 30 seconds, then add the apple, soaked raisins, vinegar and 4 tablespoons water. Bring to a boil, then turn down the heat to low and simmer 10 to 15 minutes until the liquid evaporates and the apples are soft. Stir in the sugar and half the sage. Season with a little salt, if needed, and pepper. Taste and add a little extra sugar, if required, to give a balance of sweet and tart.

4] Return the sausages to the skillet and let everything cook together for a couple of minutes, then scatter the remaining sage over the top. Serve direct from the skillet with mashed potatoes.

2 cups all-purpose flour

1/2 teaspoon salt, plus extra to taste

5 eggs

1 1/4 cups milk

6 tablespoons vegetable oil

8 good-quality link sausages, about 1 pound total weight

peas or other green vegetable, to serve

ONION GRAVY

2 tablespoons unsalted butter

2 large red onions, thinly sliced

1 small thyme sprig, leaves finely chopped

1 teaspoon all-purpose flour

1/4 cup red wine

1 1/4 cups beef stock

1 to 2 teaspoons red-currant jelly (optional)

freshly ground black pepper

SERVES 4 | **PREPARATION TIME** 20 minutes | **COOKING TIME** 1 hour 10 minutes

TOAD-IN-THE-HOLE WITH ONION GRAVY

1] To make the batter, sift the flour and salt into a bowl. Whisk the eggs and milk with 4 tablespoons water, then gradually whisk three-quarters of the mixture into the flour to make a smooth batter. Whisk in the remaining milk mixture, a little at a time, until the consistency of light cream. Transfer to a measuring jug and leave until ready to use.

2] To make the gravy, melt the butter in a large skillet over medium heat. When the butter is foaming, add the onions and thyme. Turn down the heat slightly, cover the pan and cook the onions 30 minutes, stirring frequently, until soft. Uncover the pan, increase the heat to medium and cook 10 minutes longer, stirring occasionally, until the onions caramelize slightly. Stir in the flour, then whisk in the red wine and stock. Bring to a boil, then turn down the heat and simmer 10 to 15 minutes until the gravy thickens slightly. Whisk in 1 teaspoon of the red-currant jelly, if using, adding more to taste, if you like. Season with salt and pepper and leave to one side.

3] Meanwhile, while the onions are cooking, preheat the oven to 425°F.

4] Heat 2 tablespoons of the oil in a large skillet over medium heat. Add the sausages and cook 8 to 10 minutes, turning them regularly, until golden brown all over. It is important to brown them properly, because they won't color in the batter. While the sausages are cooking, pour the remaining oil in a medium-sized roasting pan and heat in the oven 5 minutes until very hot.

5] Carefully remove the pan from the oven and put it on the stovetop over medium heat. Pour in the batter (it should start to bubble at the edges) and sit the sausages in the batter. Immediately return the pan to the oven and bake 10 minutes. Lower the oven temperature to 400°F and bake 25 to 30 minutes longer until the batter is puffy on top and crisp on the bottom. Reheat the gravy, if necessary, and serve with the "toad." I like to serve this with peas, but any green vegetable is great.

1 tablespoon olive oil

1 onion, finely chopped

1 garlic clove, crushed

2 small thyme sprigs, leaves finely chopped

½ recipe quantity (about 3 cups) Tomato Puree (see page 212)

1 pound 2 ounces lean ground pork

1 handful flat-leaf parsley leaves, finely chopped

2 tablespoons freshly shredded Grana Padano or Parmesan cheese, plus extra to serve

2 pinches ground nutmeg

14 ounces dry linguine

1 cup freshly shredded mozzarella cheese, salt and freshly ground black pepper

green salad, to serve

SERVES 4 | **PREPARATION TIME** 20 minutes, not including making the tomato puree | **COOKING TIME** 1 hour

PORK MEATBALLS WITH LINGUINE

Better than "mamma used to make," this is the perfect light lunch.

1] Preheat the oven to 350°F. Heat the oil in a large skillet over low heat. Fry the onion 8 to 10 minutes until soft and translucent. Add the garlic and thyme and cook 1 minute longer. Transfer to a large bowl and leave to cool.

2] Warm the tomato puree in a medium-sized saucepan. Season with salt and pepper.

3] Meanwhile, add the pork, parsley and cheese to the cooked onion mixture. Mix together and season with nutmeg, salt and pepper. (You can check the seasoning by frying a teaspoonful of the pork mixture in a small skillet.)

4] Form tablespoonfuls of the mixture into meatballs and put them into a baking dish. Pour the warm tomato puree over and cover the dish tightly with foil. Bake 40 to 45 minutes until the sauce is bubbling and the meatballs are cooked through.

5] Cook the linguine in a large saucepan of boiling salted water 12 minutes, or until al dente. While the pasta is cooking, preheat the broiler to high. Drain the linguine and set aside until the meatballs finish cooking. Remove the baking dish from the oven, uncover, add the drained pasta and gently toss everything together. Scatter the mozzarella over the top.

6] Put the dish under the broiler and broil 2 to 3 minutes until the mozzarella melts. Serve with extra cheese and a green salad.

JOHNNIE'S TIP

The pork mixture makes fairly firm meatballs, but if you prefer slightly softer ones, soak 2 slices crustless white bread in 4 tablespoons milk 10 minutes, then squeeze out the excess liquid. Tear the bread into small pieces and put it into the bowl with the onion mixture before adding the pork.

1¼ cups dry macaroni

2½ ounces sliced pancetta, cut into bite-size pieces

3 tablespoons unsalted butter

¼ cup all-purpose flour

3 cups milk

heaped 1 teaspoon Dijon mustard

heaped 1 cup shredded Gruyère cheese

3 tablespoons freshly shredded Parmesan cheese

cayenne pepper, to taste

2 tablespoons fresh white bread crumbs (from ½ slice of bread)

salt and ground white pepper

crisp green salad, to serve

SERVES 4 | **PREPARATION TIME** 20 minutes | **COOKING TIME** 40 minutes

PANCETTA MAC & CHEESE

Macaroni and cheese is an all-time favorite comfort food, and this version has an extra layer of taste with the addition of crisp bites of smoky pancetta.

1] Preheat the oven to 425°F. Cook the macaroni in a large saucepan of boiling salted water 10 to 12 minutes, or until al dente. Drain and rinse under cold running water, then leave to one side to drain.

2] Meanwhile, put the pancetta in a large, dry skillet over low heat. Cook 4 to 5 minutes, turning once, until the fat runs out of the pancetta. Increase the heat to medium and cook until crisp. Transfer the pancetta to a plate lined with paper towels.

3] Melt the butter in a large saucepan over low heat, then stir in the flour to make a paste. Take the pan off the heat and whisk in the milk, a little at a time, to make a smooth sauce. Return to the heat and cook, stirring constantly, until the sauce comes to a boil and thickens slightly. Turn down the heat and simmer 1 minute, stirring.

4] Remove the pan from the heat and stir in the mustard, Gruyère and Parmesan, reserving 2 tablespoons. Season to taste with cayenne, salt and pepper. Add the pancetta and cooked macaroni to the pan and stir until combined. Check the seasoning.

5] Tip the pasta and sauce into a baking dish and place on a baking sheet. Mix together the bread crumbs and the reserved Parmesan and scatter the mixture over the pasta. Bake 20 minutes until the top is golden and the sauce is bubbling. Serve with a crisp green salad.

3½ ounces prosciutto, preferably prosciutto di Parma

14 ounces dry spaghetti

4 egg yolks

1¼ cups freshly shredded Parmesan cheese, plus extra to serve

1 teaspoon olive oil

1 stick (½ cup) unsalted butter, diced

1 tablespoon finely chopped flat-leaf parsley leaves

salt and freshly grated black pepper

SERVES 4 | **PREPARATION TIME** 10 minutes | **COOKING TIME** 15 minutes

PROSCIUTTO CARBONARA

Spaghetti carbonara is a classic dish, but I have refined it here by using bite-size pieces of prosciutto and a sauce that is just a light emulsion of eggs and cheese. You can use Serrano ham instead of the prosciutto, if you like.

1] Preheat the broiler to high and line the broiler rack with foil. Broil the prosciutto 4 to 5 minutes until crisp. Leave to cool on a plate lined with paper towels, then break the prosciutto into bite-size pieces and leave to one side.

2] Meanwhile, cook the spaghetti in a large saucepan of boiling salted water 12 minutes, or until al dente.

3] Put the egg yolks and Parmesan in a bowl and whisk to combine.

4] Put the oil, butter and half of the prosciutto pieces in a large, deep skillet. Heat over medium-low heat until the butter melts.

5] Now you need to work quickly. Drain the pasta, reserving 1 cup of the cooking water. Add the cooked pasta to the skillet and turn off the heat.

6] Whisk 4 tablespoons of the pasta cooking water into the egg yolk mixture, then add to the skillet. Toss everything together with an additional 4 tablespoons of the pasta cooking water to make a thin, smooth sauce. Add a splash of extra water if the sauce is too thick. Season to taste with salt and pepper. You might not need extra salt as the ham is very salty.

7] Scatter the remaining prosciutto over the pasta and serve sprinkled with parsley and extra Parmesan.

"SHOW ME HOW" TO BROIL THE PROSCIUTTO

HOW TO ROAST PORK WITH PERFECT CRACKLINGS

You might think a roast requires lots of care and attention and, therefore, should only be cooked for a special family meal like a Sunday lunch. In reality, however, a pork loin roast is one of the easiest cuts of meat to cook and pretty much looks after itself in the oven. This is thanks to a combination of a lean "eye" of meat surrounded by a medium amount of fat. The fat melts away during roasting to keep the meat moist and gives a crisp outer rind, or cracklings. A small roast can easily be cooked for a midweek dinner, or a large roast, perhaps a rack of pork on the bone for dramatic effect, can be served for a special occasion.

The basic principle of roasting a loin of pork with perfect cracklings is that the joint is given an initial blast in a very hot oven to heat and blister the skin, setting it on its way to golden crispness. The oven temperature is then reduced to let the meat finish cooking more gently. Pork doesn't need to be roasted for a long period of time, and, in fact, if it is served slightly pink it is all the juicier and better for it.

The crowning glory of a pork roast is the crisp cracklings, the part people fight over! To create perfect cracklings is fairly straightforward, and a little touch of TLC before cooking will avoid a flabby rind. Moisture is the main enemy, because it causes the skin to steam rather than crisp. If you have the time, leave the roast in an uncovered dish in the bottom of the refrigerator for a day, making sure the raw meat does not come into contact with anything else. Alternatively, use paper towels to thoroughly pat the skin dry, or you can even give it a little blow dry with a hairdryer on a cold setting!

Next, make sure the skin is properly scored (if you have a butcher, ask him or her to do this for you). Although supermarkets tend to sell pork roasts with the skin already scored, it usually isn't cut deeply enough to get really great cracklings. If preparing the skin yourself, use a sharp, thin blade, such as a craft knife, to make long cuts into the rind; only cut into the fat and not the flesh. Make sure the cuts run parallel to each other and are spaced 1/8 to 1/4 inch apart. Scoring gives space for the fat to bubble up, basting the skin and meat. Just before cooking, rub in a little flavorless vegetable oil and season generously with coarse salt and freshly ground black pepper. The oil helps the salt to stick to the skin and the salt draws out any moisture still on the surface; any excess salt can always be brushed off after cooking.

After the pork has roasted and while it is resting, the skin can be removed and given a final blast in a hot oven or under the broiler to guarantee it properly crisps.

2 pounds boneless pork loin roast, with skin,
   tied with string
1 to 2 teaspoons vegetable oil
coarse kosher or sea salt and freshly ground
   black pepper

ROAST PORK LOIN [*pictured overleaf*]

1] Preheat the oven to 475°F and line the roasting pan with foil. Prepare the pork by drying the skin thoroughly, patting it with paper towels. Using a sharp knife, score the skin, making deep, long parallel cuts into the fat ⅛ to ¼ inch apart; do not cut into the flesh. Rub the skin with a little oil, then sprinkle pepper and a generous amount of coarse salt over the skin.

2] Sit the pork on a rack over the roasting pan and roast 25 minutes. The initial high temperature helps to promote crisp cracklings. Reduce the oven temperature to 350°F and cook the pork 45 minutes longer, turning the pan around halfway through. The meat should be slightly pink in the middle, although the juices flowing from the pork should not be bloody. If you have a meat thermometer, it should read 145°F.

3] Transfer the pork to a warm serving plate and leave to rest in a warm, draft-free place 10 to 20 minutes before carving. Don't cover the roast, because any steam coming from the resting pork can soften the cracklings. You can remove the cracklings at this point and return it to the oven, increased to 425°F, or give it a quick blast under a hot broiler to make it extra crisp. Cover the meat with foil if you remove the cracklings.

4] To carve the pork, remove the cracklings, if you haven't already done so, and cut it into strips. Carve the meat across the grain into thin slices.

JOHNNIE'S TIP

You might need to adjust the cooking times at the 350°F stage, depending on the weight of the pork roast. Allow 22 minutes per pound. If you like your pork more well done, cook 27 minutes per pound. For a bone-in rack of pork, aim for 4½-pound piece of meat to serve 4 people. Roast 25 minutes at 475°F, then turn the temperature down to 350°F and roast 18 minutes per pound.

HOME FAVORITES

4 tablespoons vegetable oil

6 sage leaves, thinly sliced

3 garlic cloves, 2 thinly sliced and 1 crushed

3 tablespoons unsalted butter, softened

4 bone-in pork loin chops, each about
   10 ounces

salt and freshly ground black pepper

1 recipe quantity Chunky Fries
   (see page 215), Wilted Spinach (see page 218)
   and lemon wedges, to serve

SERVES 4 | **PREPARATION TIME** 35 minutes | **COOKING TIME** 15 minutes

BROILED GARLIC & SAGE PORK CHOPS

Both garlic and sage are natural partners with pork, and you get a double whammy in this recipe with an infused oil and flavored butter. I love to dip my fries into the sage butter as it melts over the hot pork chop.

1] Put the oil, 4 of the sage leaves and the sliced garlic into a small saucepan. Put the pan over low heat and warm the oil until the garlic and sage just start to sizzle. Take the pan off the heat and leave the oil to infuse 30 minutes.

2] Meanwhile, put the remaining sage and the crushed garlic into a bowl and mix in the butter until combined. Put the flavored butter on a piece of plastic wrap and roll up to form a small log shape, then twist the ends to seal. Put the wrapped butter log in the freezer 10 to 15 minutes until firm.

3] Preheat the broiler to high. Brush the chops with the sage oil and season well with salt and pepper. Broil the chops 4 to 6 minutes on each side until the fat turns golden but the pork is still slightly pink in the middle.

4] Transfer the chops to warm plates. Slice the butter log into 4 and put one pat on top of each chop. Serve with chunky fries, wilted spinach and lemon wedges.

JOHNNIE'S TIP

Pork chops can be a little dry at times, but are improved by a nice long soak in a flavored brine. Dissolve 4 tablespoons salt and 4 tablespoons soft light brown sugar in ⅔ cup boiling water. Add 2 cups apple juice, 1 cup cold water, 2 sliced garlic cloves and 4 sage sprigs. Leave the brine to cool completely. Put the chops in a deep dish and pour the brine over them. Cover and refrigerate at least 8 hours, or overnight. Remove the chops from the brine and pat dry with paper towels before cooking.

1 small rosemary sprig, needles finely
   chopped, plus a few extra small sprigs

1 teaspoon sea salt

8 thin boneless pork loin chops, fat trimmed,
   each about 3–4 ounces

2 teaspoons vegetable oil

5 tablespoons unsalted butter, cubed

4 garlic cloves, very thinly sliced

a squeeze of lemon juice

freshly ground black pepper, to taste

1 recipe quantity Johnnie's Mashed Potatoes
   (see page 215), or crusty bread, and spinach,
   to serve

SERVES 4 | **PREPARATION TIME** 15 minutes | **COOKING TIME** 10 minutes

ROSEMARY & GARLIC PORK CHOPS

Pork loin chops come, as the name implies, from the hog's loin and are tender and ideal for quick-cooking techniques. Try to buy thin ones that are as lean as possible, because the very fast cooking means any fat on the meat doesn't have time to melt away.

1] Using a mortar and pestle, pound the chopped rosemary and salt together, then mix in a good grinding of pepper. Rub the chops with the oil and then the flavored salt.

2] Heat a large, dry skillet over medium-high heat 2 to 3 minutes. When you feel heat coming from the pan (hold your hand 2 inches above the pan), add the chops and cook 2 minutes on each side until brown and slightly crusted. You might need to cook them in two batches, but return them to the pan before adding the butter.

3] Add the butter to the pan and, when foaming, add the garlic and cook 1 minute, basting the steaks with the garlicky butter. Remove the pan from the heat and transfer the chops to warm plates. The pork should still be slightly pink in the middle.

4] Turn down the heat to medium and return the pan to the heat. Cook the butter and garlic 1 to 2 minutes longer until slightly brown, but watch that the garlic doesn't burn. Take the pan off the heat and stir in a squeeze of lemon juice, adding more to taste, if necessary. Spoon the butter sauce over the pork chops. Sprinkle with rosemary. Serve with mashed potatoes and spinach, but because this is such a quick dish, a hunk of crusty bread will do just as well to mop up the buttery, garlicky sauce.

JOHNNIE'S TIP:

If you can't find thin pork chops, buy 4 regular chops and cut each horizontally to make two thinner pieces. If necessary, cover the steaks with plastic wrap and beat with a wooden meat mallet or a rolling pin until they are ½ inch thick.

⅓ cup all-purpose flour

1 egg

4 boneless pork loin chops, each about
   6 ounces, fat trimmed

heaped 2 cups fresh white bread crumbs

2 tablespoons finely shredded Parmesan
   cheese

5 sage leaves

vegetable oil, for shallow frying

salt and freshly ground black pepper

lemon wedges and crisp green salad,
   to serve

SERVES 4 | **PREPARATION TIME** 30 minutes | **COOKING TIME** 10 minutes

PORK SCALLOPS IN PARMESAN CRUST

Pork makes a tempting—and much better value—alternative to the classic veal in this Milanese-style dish. If done correctly, pork produces the same, if not better, results.

1] Preheat the oven to 150°F. Put the flour on a large plate and season generously with salt and pepper. Whisk the egg in a deep dish with 1 tablespoon cold water. Line a baking sheet with paper towels.

2] Cover the pork chops with plastic wrap, then beat with a meat mallet or rolling pin until about ¼ inch thick.

3] Put the bread crumbs, Parmesan and sage in a food processor and whiz until you have fine crumbs flecked with bits of sage. Transfer the crumbs to a large plate and season with salt and pepper.

4] Pat the pork scallops dry with paper towels, then dust in the flour until well coated. Dip the scallops, one at a time, into the egg, then roll in the bread crumbs, pressing the crumbs into the pork to get a good coating.

5] Heat a thin layer of the oil in a large skillet over medium-high heat. Fry the scallops 2 minutes on each side until golden and crisp. You will need to cook them in two batches; you don't want to overcrowd the pan, because the scallops will steam rather than fry. Transfer to the lined baking sheet and keep warm in the oven while you cook the remaining scallops.

6] Serve the scallops with the lemon wedges for squeezing over and a green salad.

9 ounces fresh chorizo, cut into bite-size
   pieces
1 onion, thinly sliced
1 red bell pepper, seeded and diced
1 fat garlic clove, crushed
a pinch of saffron
1¼ cups easy-cook long-grain rice
2 cups vegetable stock, hot

⅔ cup frozen peas
8 ounces raw jumbo, shell-on shrimp
8 to 12 mussels, prepared and rinsed (discard
   any shells that remain open when tapped)
a squeeze of lemon juice
1 handful parsley leaves, roughly chopped
salt and freshly ground black pepper
lemon wedges, to serve

SERVES 4 | **PREPARATION TIME** 25 minutes | **COOKING TIME** 40 minutes

PAELLA WITH CHORIZO & SHRIMP

Long-grain rice is used in this recipe, rather than the usual short, stocky Spanish rice.
This means the rice grains stay separate when cooked, ensuring you get a little taste of
everything with each mouthful.

1] Put the chorizo in a large sauté pan over medium heat. Cook 4 to 5 minutes until
the chorizo releases its orange oil. Add the onion, pepper and garlic and cook gently
8 to 10 minutes, stirring occasionally, until soft.

2] Add the saffron and rice to the pan and stir to coat the rice in the chorizo oil. Season
with salt and pepper, then add enough of the stock to just cover the rice. Bring to a boil,
then turn down the heat to low and simmer about 15 minutes until the rice is almost
cooked but still has a slight bite. Add extra stock if the pan gets too dry, but do not stir.

3] Scatter the peas over the top and nestle the shrimp and mussels into the rice. Cook
8 to 10 minutes longer until the shrimp turn pink and curl and the mussels open.
During this time, don't stir the paella, but move the pan around over the heat
periodically so the paella cooks evenly. A crust might form on the bottom of the pan;
this is called *socorrat* and is considered a delicacy.

4] Remove any mussels that have not opened during cooking and discard them. Squeeze
a little lemon juice over and check the seasoning. Serve the paella direct from the pan
with chopped parsley scattered over the top and lemon wedges.

1¼ cups long-grain rice

2 boneless pork loin chops, each about 6 ounces, fat trimmed

a large pinch cayenne pepper

4 tablespoons soy sauce

4 tablespoons soft dark brown sugar

4 tablespoons vegetable oil

4 shallots, thinly sliced

2 garlic cloves, thinly sliced

1-inch piece gingerroot, peeled and grated

2 fresh green Thai or serrano chilies, thinly sliced

2 cups frozen peas

4 eggs

1 handful cilantro leaves, roughly chopped

4 scallions, thinly sliced

chili or hot-pepper sauce (optional), to serve

SERVES 4 | **PREPARATION TIME** 45 minutes, plus chilling | **COOKING TIME** 30 minutes

PORK WITH EGG-FRIED RICE

This is a really great variation on the Indonesian classic of *nasi goreng*, which rumor has it was enjoyed by Barack Obama during his state visit to Indonesia in 2010.

1] Put the rice in a saucepan and cover with plenty of cold water. Bring to a boil, then turn down the heat and simmer 10 minutes, or until tender. Drain and spread the rice over a large platter and leave to cool 20 minutes. Transfer the rice to a covered container and refrigerate at least 4 hours, or overnight, before using.

2] Cover the pork chops with plastic wrap and beat with a meat mallet or rolling pin until ⅛ inch thick. Cut the pork into finger-size slices. Transfer the pork slices to a bowl, dust with the cayenne pepper and leave to one side. Mix together the soy sauce and sugar, then leave to one side.

3] Heat 1 tablespoon of the oil in a large wok or skillet over medium heat. Add the shallots and fry 5 to 6 minutes until golden. Add the garlic, ginger and chilies and stir-fry 2 minutes longer. Turn up the heat to high, add the pork and stir-fry 2 to 3 minutes until the pork turns opaque, then add the cooked rice and the peas. Stir-fry 5 to 6 minutes until the peas thaw and the rice is piping hot. Stir in the soy sauce mixture, remove the wok from the heat and keep the rice warm.

4] Heat the remaining oil in a large skillet over medium heat. When shimmering, crack the eggs into the pan and fry 2 to 3 minutes until cooked to your liking.

5] Stir the cilantro into the rice and divide into 4 bowls. Sit a fried egg on top and scatter the scallions over. Serve immediately with chili sauce.

JOHNNIE'S TIP

This would also be good made using leftover Chinese Barbecue Pork (see page 133) or Korean-Style Fiery Pork (see page 130). Add at the same time as the rice, since the pork in both recipes is already cooked.

HOME FAVORITES

1 pound boneless pork loin chops, fat trimmed

1 tablespoon cornstarch

3 tablespoons ketchup

8 ounces canned pineapple rings in natural juice, drained and cut into 1/2-inch pieces, and 3 tablespoons juice reserved

1 1/2 tablespoons sweet chili sauce

1 1/2 teaspoons rice wine vinegar, plus extra to taste

1 1/2 teaspoons soft light brown sugar, plus extra to taste

2 tablespoons vegetable oil

1 red bell pepper, seeded and cut into 1/2-inch squares

1 green bell pepper, seeded and cut into 1/2-inch squares

1 bunch scallions, trimmed and cut into 3/4-inch pieces

1 garlic clove, crushed

1/4-inch piece gingerroot, peeled and finely chopped

steamed jasmine rice, to serve

SERVES 4 | **PREPARATION TIME** 20 minutes | **COOKING TIME** 10 minutes

SWEET & SOUR PORK

Sweet-and-sour pork is probably one of the most popular dishes on Chinese restaurant and carry-out menus, but it can be disappointing with heavily battered pork and a glutinous, bland sauce. My version is neither of these, with a light, crisp batter and a slightly spicy, light sauce.

1] Cover the pork chops with plastic wrap and beat with a meat mallet or rolling pin until about 1/16 inch thick. Roughly chop the pork into 1/2-inch squares and transfer to a bowl. Dust in the cornstarch and leave to one side.

2] Whisk the ketchup, canned pineapple juice, sweet chili sauce, vinegar and sugar together in a measuring jug and leave to one side.

3] Heat 1 tablespoon of the oil in a large wok or skillet over high heat. When the oil is shimmering, add the red and green peppers and the scallions and stir-fry about 4 minutes until the vegetables are soft. Transfer to a bowl and leave to one side.

4] Heat the remaining oil in the wok for a few seconds, then add the garlic and ginger and let them sizzle 30 seconds. Add the pork and stir-fry 2 minutes, or until the pork is almost cooked. Return the vegetables to the pan with the pineapple. Pour in the ketchup mixture and cook, stirring, 1 to 2 minutes until the sauce is just hot. Remove the wok from the heat and taste the sauce, adding more vinegar or sugar, if needed. Serve the pork with bowls of jasmine rice.

1¾ cups canned coconut milk

½ cup vegetable stock

¾ cup green beans, cut into 2-inch pieces

1 pound 9 ounces boneless pork loin chops,
  fat trimmed, cut into bite-size pieces

1 to 2 teaspoons fish sauce

1 to 2 teaspoons sugar

a squeeze of lime juice

1 handful cilantro leaves

thick rice noodles or steamed jasmine
  rice, to serve

THAI GREEN CURRY PASTE

2 black peppercorns

1 teaspoon cumin seeds

1 teaspoon coriander seeds

3 fresh green Thai or serrano chilies,
  roughly chopped

1 shallot, roughly chopped

2 garlic cloves, roughly chopped

stems from 1 bunch cilantro

1 handful cilantro leaves

1-inch piece galangal or ½-inch piece
  gingerroot, peeled and chopped

2 kaffir lime leaves

½ lemongrass stalk, tough outer leaves
  removed, roughly chopped

1 teaspoon fish sauce

juice of ½ lime

SERVES 4 | **PREPARATION TIME** 30 minutes | **COOKING TIME** 20 minutes

THAI GREEN CURRY WITH PORK

**You can make double the quantity of curry paste and freeze half of it for future use,
or use in the Pork & Lemongrass Wraps (see page 120).**

1] To make the Thai green curry paste, toast the peppercorns, cumin and coriander seeds
   in a dry skillet 3 to 4 minutes until fragrant. Cool slightly and grind to a powder using
   a mini food processor or mortar and pestle. Add the remaining curry paste ingredients
   and process to a coarse paste.

2] To make the curry, bring 4 tablespoons of the coconut milk to the boil in a large wok
   or deep skillet. Boil a few minutes until it separates, then add the curry paste and cook
   2 minutes longer. Stir in the rest of the coconut milk and the stock.

3] Bring to a boil, add the green beans and boil 2 minutes. Add the pork, turn down the
   heat to low and simmer the pork 5 to 6 minutes until just cooked. Don't let the curry
   boil, or the pork will become tough. Remove the wok from the heat.

4] Add 1 teaspoon each of the fish sauce and sugar and a squeeze of lime to the curry, then
   return the wok to the heat 1 minute. Taste and add more fish sauce, sugar and lime juice
   as needed. Sprinkle the curry with cilantro and serve with rice noodles.

HOME FAVORITES

1 pound boneless pork loin chops, fat trimmed

1 teaspoon paprika

2 tablespoons unsalted butter

4 shallots, thinly sliced

6 cups thinly sliced cremini mushrooms

1 fat garlic clove, crushed

2/3 cup beef stock

1 tablespoon vegetable oil

2 tablespoons brandy

1¼ cups crème fraîche or sour cream

1 teaspoon Worcestershire sauce

2 teaspoons Dijon mustard

1 small handful flat-leaf parsley leaves, chopped

salt and freshly ground black pepper

basmati or jasmine rice, to serve

SERVES 4 | PREPARATION TIME 10 minutes, plus marinating | COOKING TIME 25 minutes

PORK STROGANOFF

A kick-back to the Eighties, but with pork! It tastes just as good as the classic beef version and, of course, it's less expensive.

1] Cover the pork chops with plastic wrap and beat with a meat mallet or rolling pin until about ¼ inch thick. Cut the pork into finger-size strips and transfer to a bowl. Toss the pork in the paprika and leave to marinate at least 30 minutes.

2] Melt the butter in a large, deep skillet over medium heat. When the butter is foaming, add the shallots and cook 3 to 4 minutes until soft. Add the mushrooms and cook about 5 minutes until tender and any liquid they give off evaporates. Add the garlic and cook 1 minute longer.

3] Pour in the stock, turn up the heat to high and boil until it almost evaporates and looks syrupy. Transfer the mushroom mixture to a bowl.

4] Put the oil in the skillet and return it to high heat. When the oil is shimmering, add the pork and spread it out evenly in the pan. Season with salt and cook about 3 minutes until brown on the underside but still slightly pink on top. Stir in the brandy and either carefully flame the brandy or let it boil until it evaporates. Add the mushroom mixture and reduce the heat to very low.

5] Stir in the crème fraîche, Worcestershire sauce and mustard, then season with salt and pepper. Heat very gently until the cream is warmed through, then scatter the parsley over and serve with rice.

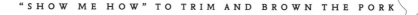

"SHOW ME HOW" TO TRIM AND BROWN THE PORK

2 tablespoons vegetable oil

1 pound 10 ounces fresh boneless pork leg, cut into 1-inch cubes

1 onion, thinly sliced

1 garlic clove, crushed

½ teaspoon ground coriander

½ teaspoon ground cumin

½-inch piece gingerroot, peeled and grated

½ teaspoon ground allspice

1 fresh red chili, seeded and diced

a pinch red pepper flakes

2 cans (15-oz.) crushed tomatoes

1 tablespoon honey

1¼ cups ready-to-eat dried apricots

1 handful cilantro leaves, finely chopped

salt and freshly ground black pepper

PISTACHIO COUSCOUS

1½ cups couscous

3 tablespoons olive oil

2 tablespoons lemon juice

⅓ cup shelled unsalted pistachios, roughly chopped

6 scallions, thinly sliced

SERVES 4 | PREPARATION TIME 20 minutes | COOKING TIME 1 hour 50 minutes

PORK & APRICOT TAGINE

What a cracker—pork with fruit is a winner every time!

1] Put 1 tablespoon of the oil in a large Dutch oven or a heavy-bottomed saucepan over medium heat. When the oil is shimmering, add the pork and cook 5 to 6 minutes, turning it regularly, until it is all brown on the outside. Transfer it to a plate and leave to one side.

2] Add the remaining oil to the casserole and cook the onion 8 to 10 minutes, stirring occasionally, until soft and slightly brown at the edges. Return the pork to the pan and stir in the garlic, ground coriander, cumin, ginger, allspice and both types of chili. Cook 2 minutes, then add the tomatoes and honey. Bring to a boil, then turn down the heat to low, cover the pan and simmer 45 minutes.

3] Uncover, add the apricots and turn up the heat slightly. Cook 45 minutes longer, uncovered, until the apricots are soft and the pork is tender, then season to taste.

4] Meanwhile, put the couscous in a bowl and cover with 1¾ cups just-boiled water. Cover and leave to stand 10 minutes until the water is absorbed. Fluff up the grains with a fork, then stir in the olive oil, lemon juice, pistachios and scallions and season. Scatter the cilantro over the tagine and serve with the couscous.

12 ready-to-eat dried prunes

6 tablespoons brandy

1 pound 2 ounces pork tenderloin, fat and silverskin membrane trimmed, cut into ½-inch-thick slices

3 tablespoons unsalted butter

1 teaspoon vegetable oil

scant 1 cup crème fraîche or sour cream

2 teaspoons Dijon mustard

a squeeze of lemon juice

2 tablespoons chopped walnuts

salt and freshly ground black pepper

1 recipe quantity Green Beans with Garlic & Almonds (see page 218) and steamed new potatoes, to serve

SERVES 4 | **PREPARATION TIME** 10 minutes, plus cooling | **COOKING TIME** 15 minutes

PORK MEDALLIONS WITH BRANDY-SOAKED PRUNES

A match made in heaven! The heavily scented aroma of the brandy infused into the prunes adds an extra dimension to this amazing dish.

1] Put the prunes in a small saucepan with 2 tablespoons of the brandy and 2 tablespoons water. Bring to a boil over medium heat, then turn down the heat and simmer 5 minutes until the prunes are soft and plump. Leave the prunes to one side to cool 20 minutes.

2] Meanwhile, cover the pork with plastic wrap and beat with a meat mallet or rolling pin until about ¼ inch thick. Season with salt and pepper.

3] Heat the butter and oil in a large skillet over high heat. When the butter is foaming, add the pork medallions and cook 2 minutes until brown and slightly crusted on the bottom, then turn over and cook another 1 minute longer.

4] Add the remaining brandy to the pan and let it boil 2 minutes until it reduces by half and the alcohol evaporates. Remove the pan from the heat and stir in the crème fraîche, mustard and prunes. Return the pan to very low heat and gently warm through the crème fraîche, making sure it doesn't boil. Season to taste with salt, pepper and a squeeze of lemon juice.

5] Spoon the prunes and the sauce over the pork medallions. Scatter the walnuts over and serve with new potatoes and green beans with garlic and almonds.

2 pieces pork tenderloin, each about 1 pound,
   fat and silverskin membrane trimmed
2 tablespoons unsalted butter
2 teaspoons vegetable oil
1 shallot, very finely chopped
1 cup dry white wine
⅔ cup vegetable stock

1 tablespoon wholegrain mustard, or to taste
6 tablespoons crème fraîche or sour cream
salt and freshly ground black pepper
1 recipe quantity Johnnie's Mashed Potatoes
   (see page 215) and Wilted Spinach (see page
   218), to serve

SERVES 4 to 6 | **PREPARATION TIME** 10 minutes | **COOKING TIME** 35 minutes

PORK TENDERLOIN WITH MUSTARD SAUCE

Pork's mild flavor is a good canvas for this punchy, grainy mustard sauce. Cook it until it is still slightly pink in the center.

1] If you like, you can trim the ends of each piece of tenderloin so they are uniform thickness with neat ends. Season generously with salt and pepper.

2] Heat the butter and oil in a large skillet over medium heat. When the butter is foaming, add the pork tenderloins and cook until brown all over, including the ends. Add the shallot and cook 2 minutes longer until slightly soft.

3] Pour the wine and stock into the pan. Bring to a boil, then turn down the heat and simmer 1 minute. Cover the pan and cook 20 minutes, turning the pork every 5 minutes. If the liquid is boiling madly, turn down the heat a little more—the pork will become stringy if it boils too hard. It should be cooked to just pink in the middle after 20 minutes. You can check this by sticking a small, sharp knife or skewer into the middle of one piece. If the juices are red, cook the pork 5 minutes longer and check again until they run clear.

4] Transfer the pork to a plate and cover with foil. Boil the liquid in the pan until it reduces by half, then turn down the heat to low. Stir in the mustard and crème fraîche and warm though for a couple of minutes without boiling.

5] Slice the pork into medallions and serve with the sauce, mashed potatoes and spinach.

JOHNNIE'S TIP

To get perfectly round medallions of pork, tie the pieces of tenderloin at 1¼-inch intervals with kitchen string. Wrap the tenderloins in plastic wrap and twist the ends, then chill overnight. Unwrap and cook the pork as in the recipe above.

"SHOW ME HOW" TO PREPARE AND COOK THE TENDERLOIN

2¾ pounds boneless pork loin roast
½ cup good-quality black olives, pitted
1¼ cups loosely packed basil leaves
¼ cup lightly toasted pine nuts
½ cup ricotta
finely grated zest of 1 lemon
1 teaspoon vegetable oil

1 teaspoon kosher or sea salt flakes
fine salt and freshly ground pepper
1 recipe quantity Creamy Gravy
  (see page 212), Goose Fat Roast
  Potatoes (see page 216) and steamed
  green beans, to serve

SERVES 4 | **PREPARATION TIME** 30 minutes, plus resting | **COOKING TIME** 1½ hours

ROLLED LOIN OF PORK WITH RICOTTA & BASIL

1] Score the skin of the pork loin at ½-inch intervals, then turn the loin over. The pork loin should have a small flap of belly that flops to one side. Turn the pork until this flap is on the right, then use a sharp knife to make a horizontal cut through the "eye" of the pork loin. Cut about three-quarters of the way through the loin, then open it out like a book. Cover in plastic wrap and beat with a meat mallet or rolling pin into a rectangular piece of pork, about ½ inch thick. Remove the plastic wrap and set aside.

2] Put the olives in a food processor with the basil leaves and pine nuts and pulse until finely chopped. Add the ricotta and lemon zest, then season and pulse again to mix.

3] Season the pork with salt and pepper, then spread the ricotta mixture on top. Roll the loin up from left to right and turn it over so the seam is underneath. Secure it by tying 4 or 5 pieces of string around the roast. Rub the oil over the skin and sprinkle with the sea salt flakes. Put the pork on a wire rack set over a roasting pan and leave to one side while you preheat the oven to 425°F.

4] Roast the pork 25 minutes, then reduce the oven temperature to 350°F and cook 1 hour longer, turning the pan around halfway through the cooking time. (If your piece of pork is a different size, cook at 350°F 22 minutes per pound after you reduce the oven temperature.) Remove the pork from the oven, transfer it to a plate and leave to rest in a warm place 20 minutes. Snip away the string and serve the pork with the creamy gravy, goose fat roast potatoes and green beans.

JOHNNIE'S TIP

For extra-crispy cracklings, turn the oven back up to 425°F when you take the pork out. Snip the string and cut off the cracklings. Put it on a baking sheet and roast 15 to 20 minutes.

"SHOW ME HOW" TO STUFF, ROLL AND TIE THE PORK LOIN

CHAPTER 2

CURED, DRIED, PRESERVED & SMOKED

There are various ways to preserve pork, many of which have been used for centuries. Curing is one method, and its big advantage when used in cooking is that it adds lots of flavor. Air-cured, or dried, hams also add a savory depth of flavor, or "umami," which brings an extra dimension to dishes, such as the Serrano Ham with Roasted Figs & Hazelnuts—the perfect blend of sweet fruit, savory meat and creamy ricotta.

When smoked, bacon and pancetta are irresistible eaten on their own. Adding them to blander ingredients, however, can completely lift a dish, such as the Pancetta & Pea Risotto or Pasta Amatriciana. The fat in these cuts can also be rendered in a hot pan and used for frying, or will keep meat moist if used as a wrapping, such as in the Bacon-Wrapped Pork with Mushroom Stuffing.

When most people think of cooked ham they think of a large roast, but smaller smoked ham hocks are inexpensive and versatile. In this chapter, the hock is used in dishes such as Ham & Pea Terrines or Ham Hock with Pinto Beans. It also infuses the cooking liquid with a delicious flavor, and can be used as a stock for the Ham Hock Broth with Kale, making a single cut of meat go a very long way.

This chapter also explains in a simple, no-fuss way how to smoke or cure your own meat with recipes for Hot-Smoked Pork Tenderloin and flavorsome Home-Cured Bacon with Maple & Juniper.

9 ounces fresh chorizo, cut into small chunks

1 red onion, minced

½ red bell pepper, seeded and finely diced

2 cans (15-oz.) crushed tomatoes

¼ teaspoon dried oregano

¼ teaspoon sugar

1 tablespoon vegetable oil

4 eggs

4 slices country-style bread, such as sourdough

chopped cilantro leaves, to serve

salt and freshly ground pepper

SERVES 4 | **PREPARATION TIME** 15 minutes | **COOKING TIME** 50 minutes

CHORIZO RANCHEROS

Huevos rancheros is a popular breakfast dish in Mexico and Spain. I like to add spicy, smoky chorizo to the tomato sauce to give it extra substance, then serve it topped with a fried egg. You can also take the more traditional route of baking the eggs in the sauce if you want to make individual portions.

1] Put the chorizo in a large, deep skillet over medium heat. Cook 4 to 5 minutes until the orange oil is released from the chorizo and is sizzling slightly. Add the onion and pepper and cook 10 minutes, stirring frequently, until soft. Add the tomatoes, oregano and sugar. Bring to a boil, then turn down the heat and simmer 25 to 30 minutes until the mixture reduces and thickens. Season to taste with salt and pepper.

2] Meanwhile, heat the vegetable oil in a separate large skillet and fry the eggs until the whites are set and the yolks remain runny. Toast the bread.

3] Spoon the sauce over the slices of toast, sit the fried eggs on top and serve sprinkled with cilantro.

20 to 22 thin smoked bacon slices

2 tablespoons unsalted butter

4 shallots, finely chopped

3 garlic cloves, crushed

3/4 teaspoon dried thyme

12 ounces pig liver, coarsely ground

12 ounces lean, boneless pork loin chops, coarsely ground

12 ounces fatback, coarsely ground

3 tablespoons brandy

3 tablespoons heavy cream

1 egg, lightly beaten

1/2 teaspoon ground allspice

1 tablespoon drained green peppercorns in brine

vegetable oil, for frying

salt and freshly ground black pepper

toast, cornichons and relish, to serve

SERVES 14 to 16 | **PREPARATION TIME** 30 minutes, plus cooling and 24 hours pressing | **COOKING TIME** 2¼ hours

ARDENNES PÂTÉ

This coarse pâté is not usually wrapped in bacon, but I like the extra flavor it adds. The pork, liver and fatback need to be coarsely ground, which is easy to do in a food processor.

1] Preheat the oven to 300°F. Line the bottom and sides of a 10- x 7¼- x 2½-inch terrine with pancetta, arranging the slices widthwise and leaving some overhang.

2] Melt the butter in a small skillet over medium heat. Add the shallots and cook 4 to 5 minutes until soft, then add the garlic and thyme and cook 1 minute longer. Transfer the mixture to a bowl and add all the remaining ingredients. Season with salt and pepper. Check the seasoning by frying a teaspoonful in a small skillet, remembering the pâté will taste less seasoned once it is cold, so you might need to add a little more than you first think.

3] Pack the pâté mixture into the terrine and fold the overhanging pieces of pancetta over the top. Cover the terrine with foil and put it in a small, deep roasting pan. Fill the roasting pan with enough water from a just-boiled kettle to come three-quarters of the way up the sides of the terrine.

4] Put the pâté in its water bath in the oven and cook 1½ hours. Uncover the pâté, top up the water if it is very low and cook 30 minutes longer. Check if the pâté is cooked through by inserting a skewer into the middle; if the juices run clear remove it from the oven. The internal temperature of the pâté should read 161°F on a meat thermometer. If it's not cooked, return to the oven 15 minutes longer and check again.

5] Remove the pâté from the water bath and leave it to cool in the terrine. When it is cool, cover with plastic wrap or foil, press by sitting a couple of cans on top and refrigerate 24 hours before turning out. Serve the pâté with toast, cornichons and your favorite relish.

10 ounces goose or duck fat

1 pound 2 ounces boneless pork shoulder or
　　Boston butt, cut into 1-inch cubes

3 tablespoons Calvados or brandy

10 black peppercorns

6 juniper berries

4 cloves

3 thyme sprigs

6 parsley sprigs

2 bay leaves

salt and freshly ground black pepper

thin slices of toast, pickled pearl onions
　　and cornichons, to serve

SERVES 8 | **PREPARATION TIME** 30 minutes, plus cooling and at least 24 hours chilling | **COOKING TIME** 4 hours

GOOSE FAT POTTED PORK

Shred cubes of slow-cooked meat to create a great, coarse-textured potted meat.

1] Melt the goose or duck fat in a medium-sized Dutch oven or a heavy-bottomed saucepan over low heat.

2] Add the pork, Calvados, peppercorns, juniper berries, cloves and the herbs, plus enough water to just cover the meat. Bring to a boil, then turn down the heat to as low as possible, cover the pan and cook 4 hours until the meat is falling apart into shreds. Check the pan regularly to make sure it is not boiling—the surface should be just trembling and you might need to top it up with extra water.

3] Remove the casserole from the heat and leave the pork to cool to room temperature, about 2 hours. Carefully lift the pieces of pork from the pan and, using 2 forks back to back, shred the meat into a bowl. Season generously with salt and pepper, because the potted pork will taste less seasoned when cold. Pack the meat into two 1¼-cup sterilized preserving jars or eight ⅔-cup ramekins. Strain the cooking liquid, discarding the spices and herbs, then spoon it over the meat to cover by about ¼ inch.

4] Cover the potted pork with a lid or plastic wrap and refrigerate until needed. The flavor will improve with keeping, so try to leave at least 24 hours before serving. (The potted pork will keep up to 1 month in the refrigerator, as long as the meat is fully covered by the fat and not exposed to the air.)

5] Remove the pork from the refrigerator about 30 minutes before serving with thin slices of toast, small pickled pearl onions and cornichons.

1 smoked ham hock, about 1 pound 10 ounces total weight

1 carrot, halved

1 onion, halved

1 celery stalk, halved

4 black peppercorns

1 bay leaf

3 or 4 parsley sprigs

½ cup frozen peas

8 cornichons, finely chopped

1 handful flat-leaf parsley leaves, finely chopped

8 slices prosciutto, preferably prosciutto di Parma

freshly ground black pepper

thin slices of toast, to serve

SERVES 4 | **PREPARATION TIME** 20 minutes, plus cooling and overnight chilling | **COOKING TIME** 4½ hours

HAM & PEA TERRINES

Peas and ham have a natural affinity, and these little terrines make an attractive light summer lunch.

1] Put the ham hock, carrot, onion and celery in a large saucepan and pour in enough cold water to cover by ¾ inch (about 8 cups). Bring to a boil over medium heat, skimming off any foamy scum that rises to the surface. Turn down the heat to low.

2] Add the peppercorns, bay leaf and parsley stems, then part-cover with a lid and simmer very gently 4 hours, or until the ham starts to fall away from the bone. Transfer the ham to a plate and leave to cool.

3] Strain the cooking liquid through a fine strainer into a clean saucepan, discarding the vegetables, peppercorns, bay leaf and parsley sprigs. Put the pan over medium heat and boil until it reduces to 1¼ cups. Leave to one side to cool.

4] Meanwhile, boil the peas 1 minute, then drain and refresh under cold running water. Drain again and leave to one side.

5] Pull the meat away from the bone, discarding any fat and skin. Tear the ham into small pieces and put it in a large bowl with the peas, cornichons and chopped parsley. Season with pepper, but don't use salt as the reduced cooking liquid has enough seasoning.

6] Line 4 x 1-cup ramekins with the prosciutto, leaving some overhang. Divide the ham mixture between the ramekins, pressing it down firmly. Add just enough of the reduced liquid to cover the ham mixture, then fold the prosciutto over the top to cover the surface and chill 1 hour. Cover each ramekin with plastic wrap, put a small weight on top (you can use other ramekins or small coffee cups filled with baking beans) and refrigerate overnight.

7] To serve, run a knife around the rim of each terrine and turn out onto a plate. Serve with slices of toast.

CURED, DRIED, PRESERVED & SMOKED

5 eggs

8 slices white bread (thin or medium)

8 slices prosciutto, preferably
   prosciutto di Parma

8 sun-blush tomatoes, sliced, or sun-dried
   tomatoes in oil, drained and sliced

8 ounces fresh mozzarella cheese, drained and
   cut into ¼-inch-thick slices

8 basil leaves

3 tablespoons unsalted butter, plus extra,
   if needed

salt and freshly ground black pepper

2 handfuls arugula leaves, to serve

SERVES 4 | **PREPARATION TIME** 10 minutes | **COOKING TIME** 15 minutes

PROSCIUTTO, MOZZARELLA & SUN-BLUSH TOMATOES IN CARROZZA

This *carrozza* is the ultimate toasted sandwich and there isn't any need for an electric sandwich maker! The filling is a great mix of sweet tomatoes, salty prosciutto and unctuous mozzarella—perfect.

1] Break the eggs into a shallow dish, season with salt and pepper and whisk until frothy.

2] Set out 4 slices of bread and lay 2 slices of prosciutto on each, folding the ham to fit and leaving a small border of bread around the edges. Top with the tomatoes and mozzarella in a single layer (you might not need all of the cheese, depending on the size of the bread). Sit the basil leaves on the mozzarella. Brush a little of the beaten egg over the edges of the bread, then top with a second slice of bread, pressing down firmly. (If you are being fancy, you can remove the crusts, or even cut each sandwich into a large circle using a round cutter.)

3] Melt the butter in a large skillet over medium heat. Dip each sandwich in the beaten egg, turning until coated.

4] When the butter is foaming, gently slide 2 sandwiches into the pan, ham-side down. Fry 2 to 3 minutes until golden on the underside. Using a metal spatula, carefully turn the sandwiches over and fry 3 minutes longer until golden brown on both sides. Repeat with the remaining sandwiches, adding more butter if necessary. Turn down the heat if the bread is browning too quickly, because the cheese needs to be given time to heat through and melt. Serve the sandwiches with arugula leaves.

HOW TO SMOKE PORK

Home-smoking isn't as challenging as it sounds, and it is even possible to make your own smoker from ordinary kitchen equipment. It's basically no more than a container with a lid—you can use a covered charcoal barbecue, a wok or even buy a simple smoker. If you want to try smoking without investing much money, however, it's feasible to make a basic smoker from a small roasting pan, a rack and aluminum foil.

Special smoking wood chips are required, and you need to make sure they are free of pesticides, as well as cut into small chips that will smoke for a long amount of time. The type of wood can be varied to give different flavors and many are now available to buy online.

Cooking times depend on the cut of the meat—a large piece can take several hours, while a smaller piece of tenderloin can be done quickly, but both taste great with a fragrant smokiness.

---

2 pieces pork tenderloin, about 1 pound each, fat and silverskin membrane trimmed
2 teaspoons smoked paprika
2 teaspoons soft light brown sugar
1/2 teaspoon dried oregano

1/2 teaspoon salt
1/4 teaspoon ground black pepper

YOU WILL ALSO NEED
smoking chips, preferably hickory

SERVES 4 | **PREPARATION TIME** 30 minutes, plus marinating and overnight cooling | **COOKING TIME** 20 minutes

HOT-SMOKED PORK TENDERLOIN

1] Put the pork pieces on a large piece of plastic wrap. Mix together the smoked paprika, sugar, oregano, salt and pepper and rub the mixture over the pork. Wrap the pork tightly in the plastic wrap and leave to marinate in the refrigerator 8 hours, or overnight.

2] To make a stovetop smoker, you need a medium-sized, heavy-bottomed roasting pan with a wire rack that fits inside; a broiler pan is ideal. Cover the bottom with a layer of smoking chips (you can line the pan with foil to protect it) and sit the wire rack on top. Put the pork pieces on the rack and cover with a double layer of foil, making sure it is sealed very tightly around the edges to keep in the smoke.

3] Put the smoker over high heat 3 to 4 minutes. When you see the odd wisp of smoke, turn the heat to low and cook 12 minutes. Turn off the heat and leave to stand 2 minutes before opening the foil. The pork should be cooked through, but if it is very pink and bloody in the middle, you will need to pan-fry the pieces 8 to 10 minutes. Leave the pork to cool, then cover and refrigerate overnight before serving thinly sliced as part of a charcuterie platter. The meat will keep up to 4 days in the refrigerator.

⅓ cup hazelnuts

4 large or 8 small figs

2 teaspoons honey

½ cup mascarpone

1 to 2 tablespoons milk

8 slices Serrano ham, about 3½ ounces total weight

1 handful arugula leaves

2 tablespoons hazelnut or extra virgin olive oil

juice of ½ lemon

salt and freshly ground pepper

country-style bread, lightly charred on a grill pan, to serve (optional)

SERVES 4 (as an appetizer) | PREPARATION TIME 15 minutes | COOKING TIME 35 minutes

SERRANO HAM WITH ROASTED FIGS & HAZELNUTS

A perfect combination of taste and texture—sweet figs and salty ham, with a crunch from the hazelnuts.

1] Preheat the oven to 300°F. Put the hazelnuts on a baking sheet in a single layer and toast 20 to 25 minutes until lightly brown. You should just start to smell a hazelnut aroma. Remove the nuts from the oven and increase the temperature to 425°F.

2] If the hazelnuts have their skins on, transfer them to a clean dish towel and rub vigorously until the skins come off. Using a rolling pin, roughly crush the nuts, then leave to one side.

3] Cut a cross in the top of each fig, cutting about halfway down toward the bottom. Stand the figs upright on a baking sheet and drizzle the honey over. Roast 5 to 10 minutes until the figs warm through and soften a little. The timing will depend on the ripeness of your figs—riper ones soften very quickly.

4] Mix half of the hazelnuts with the mascarpone, adding the milk to soften the mixture slightly. Put it in a pot or bowl ready to serve.

5] Serve the ham with the figs, then scatter the remaining hazelnuts and the arugula leaves over. Drizzle the oil and lemon juice over the top, then season with salt and pepper. Serve with the mascarpone cream and slices of chargrilled bread, if you like.

1 smoked ham hock, about 2 pounds 4 ounces
   total weight

1 large onion, quartered

2 celery stalks, halved

5 carrots, 2 scrubbed and halved and 3 cut
   into large dice

6 black peppercorns

4 thyme sprigs

2 bay leaves

4 garlic cloves

1½ cups shredded kale

2 ounces dry capellini or similar thin noodles,
   such as vermicelli

freshly ground black pepper

extra virgin olive oil or cold-pressed canola oil
   and crusty bread, to serve

SERVES 6 | **PREPARATION TIME** 20 minutes | **COOKING TIME** 4½ hours

HAM HOCK BROTH WITH KALE

Ham hock, one of the few bargain cuts of meat still available, is the shin part of the leg, which is smoked in a similar way to bacon. Here, nothing goes to waste, because the cooking liquid becomes the broth base for this comforting soup.

1] Put the ham hock in a large saucepan and cover with 5 quarts cold water. Add the onion, celery, 2 of the carrots, peppercorns, thyme and bay leaves. Bruise the garlic cloves by crushing them slightly with the back of a knife and add these, too.

2] Bring to a boil over high heat, skimming off any foamy scum that rises to the surface. Turn down the heat to low, then simmer the ham hock very gently 4 hours, uncovered, until the meat starts to fall away from the bone. Continue to skim the surface of the cooking liquid occasionally.

3] Remove the ham hock from the pan and strain the cooking liquid into a clean pan. Bring to a boil over high heat and boil until the liquid reduces by about one-third (you need about 8 cups stock). Add the remaining carrots and kale, turn down the heat and simmer 20 minutes until the vegetables are tender.

4] Break the pasta into the soup and cook 3 to 5 minutes until al dente. Season the soup with pepper (you shouldn't need any salt). Drizzle with a little olive oil and serve with crusty bread.

3 tablespoons unsalted butter

3 large white sweet onions, thinly sliced

3/4 ounce sage sprigs, plus 12 leaves

2 Yukon Gold potatoes, about 12 ounces total weight, peeled

2 1/4 cups vegetable stock

4 tablespoons heavy cream

salt and ground white pepper

soft white rolls, to serve

BEIGNETS

1/2 cup all-purpose flour

1/2 cup cornstarch

1/4 teaspoon salt

2/3 cup brown ale

vegetable oil, for deep frying

2 slices blood sausage, about 4 ounces total weight, casing removed and diced

SERVES 4 | PREPARATION TIME 40 minutes | COOKING TIME 1 hour 10 minutes

SAGE & ONION SOUP WITH BLOOD SAUSAGE BEIGNETS

The blood sausage "doughnuts" burst in your mouth when you bite into them—beautiful!

1] Melt the butter in a large saucepan over very low heat. Add the onions and sage sprigs and cover the pan. Cook very gently 40 minutes, stirring occasionally, until the onions are very soft and sweet.

2] Remove the sage sprigs and add the potatoes, stock and 1/2 cup water. Bring to a boil, then turn down the heat and simmer about 25 minutes until the potatoes are very soft.

3] Meanwhile, make the beignets. Sift the flour and cornstarch into a bowl with the salt. Stir in the ale with a fork to make a batter; don't worry if there are a few lumps.

4] Pour enough oil into a large saucepan or a deep-fat fryer to fill by one-third. Heat the oil to 350°F. Drop the pieces of blood sausage into the batter and lift out with a fork, then transfer to the hot oil. Fry a few at a time 4 minutes until golden brown, turning them carefully halfway. Transfer the beignets to a plate lined with paper towels to drain. You will need to cook the beignets in 2 or 3 batches to avoid overcrowding the pan.

5] Fry the sage leaves in the hot oil 20 seconds until crisp, then transfer to the plate lined with paper towels to drain.

6] Using a hand blender or food processor, puree the soup until smooth. Stir in the cream and season with salt and white pepper. Gently reheat the soup, if necessary, making sure it doesn't boil. Serve the soup with the beignets sitting in the middle and topped with the sage leaves. Serve immediately with soft white rolls.

1 recipe quantity Gnocchi (see page 214), made
   with 1½ teaspoons freshly ground
   black pepper
4 tablespoons unsalted butter
9 ounces blood sausage, casing removed,
   sliced and quartered

16 sage leaves
1 teaspoon white wine vinegar
4 very fresh extra-large eggs
salt and freshly ground black pepper

SERVES 4 | **PREPARATION TIME** 2 hours (including making the gnocchi) |
COOKING TIME 15 minutes

GNOCCHI WITH BLOOD SAUSAGE & POACHED EGGS

Pan-frying gnocchi to create an outer "crust" and soft middle adds another dimension
to this already fabulous dish. You might find it easier to parcook the poached eggs
by cooking them just until the outside of the whites set, then transferring them to a bowl
of ice-cold water. You can then reheat them in boiling water just before serving.

1] Make the gnocchi following the recipe directions on page 214, adding 1½ teaspoons
ground black pepper to the dough at the same time as the egg and salt (in step 3). Put
the prepared gnocchi on baking sheets lined with waxed paper and dusted with flour,
then leave to one side.

2] Bring a large saucepan of salted water to a boil. Meanwhile, melt the butter in a large
skillet over medium heat. When the butter is foaming, add the blood sausage and fry
3 to 4 minutes until the edges start to crisp. Remove the skillet from the heat.

3] Put the gnocchi into the pan of boiling water and return it to a boil, then turn down
the heat and simmer about 4 minutes until cooked. Just before the gnocchi are cooked,
return the skillet to medium heat. Using a slotted spoon, remove the gnocchi from the
water and blot any excess water with paper towels before adding them to the skillet. Add
the sage leaves and cook 1 to 2 minutes, adding a splash of the gnocchi cooking water
to give a bit of extra moisture. Cover the pan and keep warm.

4] Bring a large pan of water to a boil and add the vinegar. Crack the eggs, one at a time,
into the pan and poach them about 2 minutes until the whites are set and the yolks are
still runny. Serve the gnocchi and blood sausage topped with a poached egg. Season
with extra black pepper before serving.

1 recipe quantity Gnocchi (see page 214)
8 slices Serrano ham
4 basil sprigs

PESTO
3 tablespoons pine nuts
4 large handfuls basil leaves
½ cup olive oil
2 tablespoons freshly shredded Grana Padano
    cheese, plus extra to serve
1 tablespoon lemon juice
salt and freshly ground black pepper

SERVES 4 | **PREPARATION TIME** 2 hours (including making the gnocchi) |
COOKING TIME 15 minutes

GNOCCHI WITH PESTO & SERRANO HAM

**Pesto, pesto, pesto! So simple to make, so awful to buy—you really will not believe
the difference.**

1] Make the gnocchi following the recipe instructions on page 214. Put the prepared
gnocchi on baking sheets lined with waxed paper and dusted with flour, then leave
to one aside.

2] To make the pesto, toast the pine nuts in a dry skillet over low heat, then leave to
one side to cool completely. Use a hand blender to whiz the basil leaves and oil 2 to
3 minutes to make a smooth, bright green oil. Crush the cooled pine nuts with the back
of a large knife or the heel of your hand and fold them into the basil oil with the cheese.
Add the lemon juice to slightly cut the oiliness of the sauce, then season to taste with
salt and pepper. (You can make the basil oil in a blender or food processor, but stir the
pine nuts, cheese and lemon juice in by hand, because the heat from the blades can
affect the flavor.)

3] Bring a large saucepan of salted water to a boil. Meanwhile, put the Serrano ham into
a large, dry skillet set over low heat. Cook the ham 3 to 4 minutes, turning once, until
crisp. Break up 4 of the ham slices, leave them in the skillet and set the remaining slices
to one side.

4] Put the gnocchi into the pan of salted water and return to a boil, then reduce the heat
and simmer about 4 minutes until cooked. Using a slotted spoon, remove the gnocchi
from the water and blot any excess water with paper towels before adding them to the
skillet. Add the pesto and toss the gnocchi, ham and pesto together.

5] Serve the gnocchi and sauce topped with the reserved wafers of crisp Serrano ham and
basil sprigs, with extra cheese sprinkled over.

12 large sea scallops, ½- to ¾-inch thick

3 tablespoons extra virgin olive oil

1 tablespoon lemon juice

2 tablespoons vegetable oil

10 ounces boudin noir or blood sausage, casing removed and cut into 12 x ½-inch-thick slices

2 large handfuls arugula leaves

salt and freshly ground black pepper

baguette, to serve

SERVES 4 | **PREPARATION TIME** 15 minutes | **COOKING TIME** 10 minutes

SEARED SCALLOPS WITH BOUDIN NOIR

Scallops and French boudin noir, or blood sausage, is a really classic combination. It is worth searching out good-quality blood sausage, because it has a much smoother texture and superior flavor to the prepacked, sliced alternative.

1] Remove the roe and any hard connective tissue from the scallops. Pat the scallops dry but do not season them at this stage, because the salt will draw out moisture.

2] Whisk the olive oil, lemon juice, salt and pepper together in a nonmetallic bowl and leave to one side.

3] Put a plate in a warm place and line a second plate with paper towels. Heat the vegetable oil in a large, heavy-bottomed skillet over high heat. Hold your hand about 6 inches above the pan; if you can feel the heat, the pan is ready to use. Add the scallops and cook 1 to 2 minutes until caramelized on the bottom, then turn over and cook 1 to 1½ minutes longer. By this time they should be just cooked in the middle. Don't overcook the scallops or they will become dry and lose their sweetness.

4] Transfer the scallops to the warm plate and cover with foil. Add the boudin noir to the skillet. Cook 1½ to 2 minutes on each side until slightly crusted, then transfer to the lined plate and pat with paper towels. Season the scallops with salt and pepper.

5] Whisk the olive oil dressing again and toss with the arugula leaves. Serve the arugula topped with the scallops and boudin noir, and with slices of baguette.

1¼ cups dry pinto beans

1 smoked ham hock, about 2¼ pounds
  total weight

1 celery stalk, halved

1 large carrot, scrubbed and halved

1 large onion, quartered

6 black peppercorns

2 bay leaves

6 parsley sprigs

1 tablespoon olive oil

1 onion, finely chopped

1 fat garlic clove, crushed

2 cans (15-oz.) crushed tomatoes

1 tablespoon Dijon mustard

½ cup dark turbinado sugar

½ teaspoon dried oregano

salt and freshly ground black pepper

a few cilantro leaves and cornbread,
  to serve

SERVES 4 to 6 | **PREPARATION TIME** 30 minutes, plus overnight soaking |
COOKING TIME 5½ hours

HAM HOCK & PINTO BEANS

Yeeeehaaaaa—cowboy beans with style!

1] Put the beans in a large bowl and cover with water. Leave to soak overnight.

2] Put the ham hock in a large saucepan or stockpot and cover with cold water. Add the celery, carrot, quartered onion, peppercorns, bay leaves and parsley sprigs. Bring to a boil, then turn down the heat and simmer, partially covered, 4 hours until the meat starts to fall away from the bone.

3] About 30 minutes before the ham is cooked, drain the beans. Put the beans in a large saucepan and cover with fresh cold water, then bring to a boil over high heat and boil rapidly 10 minutes. Drain the beans.

4] Remove the ham hock from the pan and reserve 1 cup of the cooking liquid. Remove the meat in large chunks from the ham hock and discard any skin or fat.

5] Heat the oil in a large saucepan over medium heat and cook the chopped onion and garlic 8 to 10 minutes until soft. Add the drained beans, tomatoes, mustard, sugar and oregano, plus ½ cup of the reserved ham cooking liquid. Bring to a boil, then turn the heat down to a simmer.

6] Add the chunks of ham and simmer 1 to 1¼ hours until the beans are tender. Stir occasionally, taking care not to break the ham up too much and adding extra cooking liquid, if necessary. Season with pepper and salt, if needed. Serve scattered with a few cilantro leaves, and with wedges of cornbread.

5½ cups peeled and coarsely grated
  Yukon Gold potatoes
1 onion, coarsely grated
½ teaspoon salt
1 tablespoon all-purpose flour
vegetable oil, for frying
1 pint cherry tomatoes

4 tablespoons olive oil
¼ teaspoon sugar
4 thick slices Black Forest ham, honey-baked
  ham or other baked ham of your choice,
  about 10 ounces total weight
salt and freshly ground black pepper

SERVES 4 | **PREPARATION TIME** 30 minutes | **COOKING TIME** 20 minutes

RÖSTIS WITH HONEY-BAKED HAM & TOMATOES

A rösti with a well-cooked, crisp outer and a soft potato middle is your goal. If this is achieved, I guarantee the whole dish will sing sweetly when devoured! If you want to make one large rösti, use a 12-inch skillet and cook about 15 minutes on each side until golden.

1] Put the potatoes and onion into a large colander. Toss with the salt and leave to drain 30 minutes. Transfer to a clean dish towel. Bring the edges of the towel together and twist tightly, squeezing out as much water from the potato mixture as possible. Transfer the potato mixture to a large bowl, then mix in the flour and season with a little pepper.

2] Preheat the oven to 425°F. Line a baking sheet with paper towels.

3] Heat a thin layer of vegetable oil in a large skillet over medium heat. Put one-quarter of the potato mixture in the pan and spread it out to a thin circle, about 6 inches in diameter. Repeat to cook two röstis at a time. Fry the röstis 4 to 5 minutes on each side until golden and crisp. Turn down the heat slightly if the outside is browning too quickly. Transfer the röstis to the lined baking sheet and cover with foil to keep warm while you cook the remainder.

4] While the röstis are cooking, put the tomatoes in a baking tray, drizzle with the olive oil and sprinkle the sugar over. Season with a little salt and pepper. Roast the tomatoes 8 to 10 minutes until soft and the skins just start to split.

5] Serve the röstis topped with a slice of ham and the roasted tomatoes.

10 ounces fingerling potatoes

2 tablespooons unsalted butter, plus extra for greasing

1 bunch scallions, thinly sliced

9 ounces good-quality cooked ham, cut into bite-size pieces

4 ounces shelled, cooked large shrimp

2/3 cup crumbled feta cheese

6 eggs

4 tablespoons heavy cream

2 tablespoons chopped dill

salt and freshly ground black pepper

green salad, to serve

SERVES 4 to 6 | **PREPARATION TIME** 15 minutes | **COOKING TIME** 1 hour

HAM, SHRIMP & FETA FRITTATA

A well-made, flavorsome frittata that makes a satisfying lunchtime meal.

1] Put the potatoes in a large saucepan of salted water. Bring to a boil, then turn down the heat slightly and simmer 15 to 20 minutes until just tender. Drain the potatoes and spread them out on a baking sheet to cool to room temperature.

2] Meanwhile, preheat the oven to 350°F. Cut a circle of parchment paper about 12 inches in diameter. Grease the bottom and side of a medium-sized skillet with an ovenproof handle. Press the parchment paper into the bottom of the pan and up the side; the butter should help it stick. Lining the skillet means your frittata will turn out cleanly without sticking to the pan.

3] Cut the potatoes into 1/2-inch-thick slices. Melt the butter in a separate large skillet over high heat. When it is foaming, add the potatoes and fry 4 minutes, turning occasionally, until golden. Add the scallions and cook 1 minute, then remove the pan from the heat and spread the potato mixture over the paper in the skillet. Scatter the ham, shrimp and feta over the potatoes, pressing them down slightly.

4] Whisk the eggs, cream and dill together in a measuring jug. Season with a pinch of salt and plenty of pepper. Pour the egg mixture into the pan, shaking it slightly to distribute the egg evenly. Bake the frittata 25 to 30 minutes, turning the pan halfway through, until the frittata is just set in the middle.

5] Remove the pan from the oven and turn out the frittata. The easiest way to do this is to put a large heatproof plate or board over the top of the skillet, then flip it over so the frittata drops onto the plate. Take care when you do this, because the pan will be very hot. Peel the paper off immediately to prevent the frittata becoming soggy. Serve hot or cold, cut into wedges and with a green salad.

vegetable oil, for greasing

4 smoked ham steaks, each about 7 ounces

2 tablespoons unsalted butter

1 tablespoon sugar

2 large firm eating apples, such as Pink Lady, peeled, cored and each cut into 6 wedges

4 handfuls watercress

1 recipe quantity Creamy Garlic Potatoes (see page 216), to serve

SERVES 4 | **PREPARATION TIME** 10 minutes | **COOKING TIME** 15 minutes

HAM WITH CARAMELIZED APPLES

Streets away from the traditional ham and pineapple, this simple dish is great to eat at any time of the day, from a light lunch to a late supper.

1] Preheat the oven to its lowest setting. Heat a ridged, cast-iron grill pan or skillet over medium heat and brush with a little oil. Cook the ham steaks 3 to 4 minutes on each side until cooked through. Transfer them to the oven to keep warm while you cook the apples.

2] Put a medium-sized skillet over low heat. Add the butter and sugar and and heat until the butter melts, then turn up the heat to high and bubble 1 minute. Add the apples and cook 4 to 5 minutes, turning halfway, until the caramel starts to turn dark amber and is smoking slightly. Take the pan off the heat and keep turning the apples in the caramel 2 minutes.

3] Spoon the caramelized apple slices and sauce over the ham steaks and serve with a handful of watercress and creamy garlic potatoes.

JOHNNIE'S TIP

If your ham steaks come with a rind, use kitchen scissors to snip the fat at ¼-inch intervals to prevent the steaks curling during cooking.

HOW TO CURE BACON

Although bacon is a firm favorite with many people, much of the mass-market produce falls far short of its potential due to the curing process. Curing might sound complicated, but it really isn't—it's just a simple process of preserving meat using salt. Low-grade bacon comes from curing in a salty solution or brine, which results in a lot of excess water in the meat, leaving it flabby and tasteless.

The best method is to dry-cure bacon, using a simple mix of salt and spices. This draws the water out of the pork and leaves only the quality meat and fat, resulting in tastier bacon and one that crisps really well when cooked. Regular kosher or sea salt is perfectly effective for the curing process, and pork belly is the easiest cut to cure, because it is a manageable size and shape—also, it will only take about 1 week to cure at home.

2¼ pounds pork belly, skin on
½ cup coarse kosher or sea salt
4 juniper berries, crushed

2 tablespoons soft light brown sugar
2 tablespoons maple syrup

SERVES 8 | **PREPARATION TIME** 20 minutes, plus 5 days curing and at least 24 hours drying

HOME-CURED BACON WITH MAPLE & JUNIPER

1] Put the pork belly on a cutting board and pat it dry with paper towels. Mix together the salt, juniper berries, sugar and maple syrup and rub this all over the pork, making sure you get it into any crevices in the meat. Transfer the meat to a heavy-duty, resealable freezer bag and add any salt mixture left on the cutting board. Squeeze as much air as possible out of the bag and seal it tightly.

2] Put the bag into a nonmetallic dish, so the meat is sitting skin-side up, and put it in the bottom of the refrigerator. Leave 5 days, turning the bag over once a day.

3] After 5 days, take the bacon out of the bag and rinse thoroughly in cold water. Pat dry with paper towels and place on a wire rack to dry, uncovered, in a cool place at least 24 hours (or leave it a couple of days, if you prefer). The refrigerator is too humid, so try to find a cool garage or other cool, dry place to use. You can cover the bacon with a piece of cheesecloth while it is drying, which allows the air to circulate. Slice the bacon thinly before cooking.

"SHOW ME HOW" TO CURE THE BACON

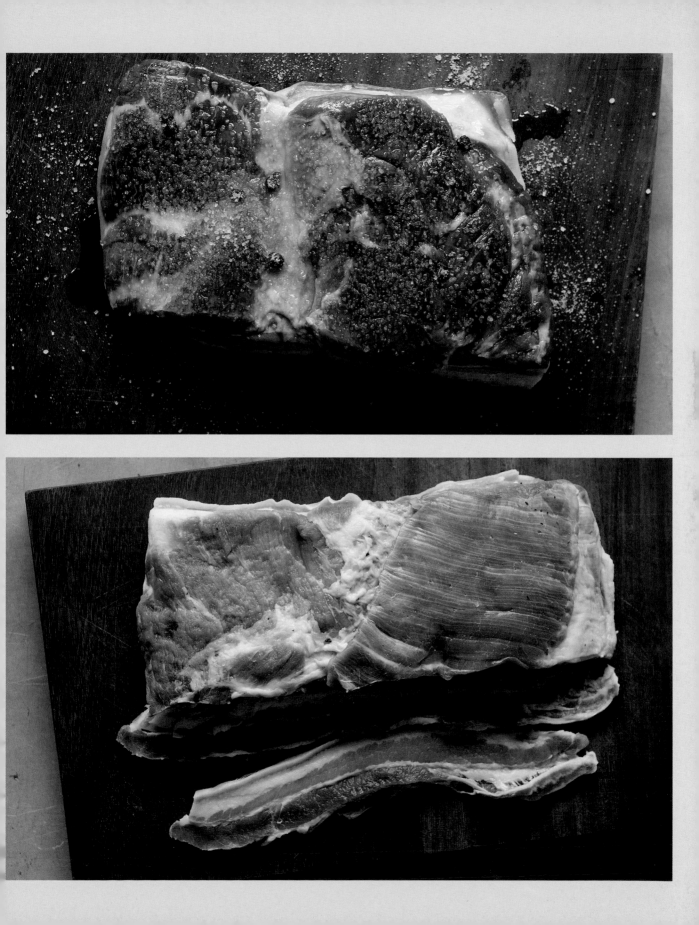

2 tablespoons unsalted butter

1 large onion, thinly sliced

1 garlic clove, crushed

7 ounces lardons, cubetti di pancetta or diced thick smoked bacon

heaped 3 cups baby button mushrooms

½ cup dry white wine

¾ cup heavy cream

scant 1 cup freshly shredded Swiss cheese

salt and freshly ground black pepper

boiled fingerling potatoes or crusty bread and crisp green salad, to serve

SERVES 4 | **PREPARATION TIME** 10 minutes | **COOKING TIME** 40 minutes

LARDON & MUSHROOM GRATIN

Ian Boasman, former owner of *Bistro French*, in Preston, England, taught me how to cook this cracking little dish; he used to call it "Magic Mushrooms" on his menu!

1] Melt half the butter in a large skillet over low heat. Add the onion and garlic and cook 10 to 15 minutes, stirring occasionally, until soft and just starting to turn a golden color.

2] Meanwhile, put the lardons in a medium-sized saucepan and just cover with cold water. Bring to a simmer over medium heat, then drain and repeat the process. Drain again and leave the lardons in a strainer until needed.

3] Using a slotted spoon, scoop the onion and garlic onto a plate and leave to one side. Add the lardons to the skillet and cook over medium heat 5 to 6 minutes until crisp. Transfer to a bowl.

4] Melt the remaining butter in the skillet and, when foaming, cook the mushrooms 8 to 10 minutes until golden brown. Return the onion and garlic to the pan and tip in the wine. Bring to a boil and cook until the wine reduces down to a syrupy liquid. Add the cream and boil again 2 to 3 minutes until thick—it should leave a slight ribbon trail when you lift a spoon out of the sauce.

5] Meanwhile, preheat the broiler to high. Remove the pan from the heat and stir in the lardons, then season to taste with salt and pepper. Tip the creamy mixture into a flameproof dish, or 4 individual gratin dishes, and sprinkle the Swiss cheese over. Broil the gratin 3 minutes, or until the cheese melts and is bubbling and tinged with brown in places. Serve immediately with boiled potatoes or crusty bread and a green salad.

JOHNNIE'S TIP

If the lardons are smoked, I prefer to blanch them first to reduce their saltiness (see page 30), but you can use a mild-cured, unsmoked pork belly instead. Cut the belly into lardons and omit the blanching, then cook before the onion until crisp. Remove from the pan, then cook the onion in the pork fat left in the pan.

7 ounces lardons, cubetti di pancetta or diced thick smoked streaky bacon

1 red onion, minced

1 red bell pepper, seeded and very finely diced

1 zucchini, very finely diced

2 fresh small red dried chilies, thinly sliced, or ½ teaspoon red pepper flakes

1 cup Tomato Puree (see page 212)

14 ounces dry, ridged pasta, such as penne rigate, rigatoni or lumaconi

2 tablespoons freshly shredded Parmesan cheese, plus extra to serve

1 small handful flat-leaf parsley leaves, finely chopped

salt and freshly ground black pepper

green salad, to serve

SERVES 4 | **PREPARATION TIME** 15 minutes | **COOKING TIME** 35 minutes

PASTA AMATRICIANA

I like to add finely diced vegetables to this spicy amatriciana sauce. They are fried until golden and almost caramelized, so they add an extra dimension to the spicy, smoky sauce. The ridges on the pasta help the sauce cling to it, so every mouthful is packed full of flavor.

1] Put the lardons in a large, deep skillet over low heat. Cook 8 to 10 minutes until the fat melts out of them. Turn up the heat to medium and cook about 5 minutes longer until the lardons are crisp. Using a slotted spoon, scoop the lardons onto a plate, leaving the fat in the pan.

2] Add the vegetables to the skillet and fry over medium heat 10 to 15 minutes, stirring frequently, until they are brown at the edges. Take care toward the end of the cooking time, because they can burn easily. Add the chilies and cook 1 minute, then stir in the tomato puree. Bring to a boil, then turn down the heat and simmer 2 minutes.

3] Meanwhile, cook the pasta in a large pan of boiling salted water 12 minutes, or until al dente. Drain, reserving 1 cup of the cooking water. Add the cooked pasta to the skillet and toss it in the sauce, adding a few splashes of the pasta cooking water if the sauce is too thick; it should lightly coat the pasta. Sprinkle the Parmesan over and season with salt and pepper. Sprinkle the pasta with the parsley and serve with extra cheese and a green salad.

12 thin smoked bacon slices

2 shallots, finely chopped

2 fat garlic cloves, crushed

1 cup fresh bread crumbs, preferably from an Italian loaf, such as ciabatta or Pugliese

2 tablespoons freshly shredded Grana Padano cheese

finely grated zest of 1 lemon

1 large handful parsley leaves, finely chopped

6 tablespoons vegetable or chicken stock

4 boneless pork loin chops, each about 6 ounces, fat trimmed

2 tablespoons vegetable oil

salt and freshly ground black pepper

1 cup Tomato Puree (see page 212)

boiled fingerling potatoes and green salad, to serve

SERVES 4 | **PREPARATION TIME** 25 minutes | **COOKING TIME** 35 minutes

ITALIAN PORK ROLLS

1] Leave to one side 8 slices of the bacon and roughly chop the remainder. Cook the chopped bacon in a large, dry skillet over low heat 3 to 4 minutes until the fat starts to run. Add the shallots and garlic and cook 8 to 10 minutes, stirring occasionally, until soft. Turn up the heat to medium-high and cook 2 minutes longer, stirring, until golden.

2] Put the bacon mixture into a bowl and leave to cool, then stir in the bread crumbs, Grana Padano, lemon zest and parsley. Add the stock, 1 tablespoon at a time, until the mixture is just moist enough to bind together, then season with a little salt and pepper.

3] Cut the pork chops in half horizontally through the middle. Lay the pieces out on a large chopping board and cover with plastic wrap, then beat with a meat mallet or rolling pin until $1/16$ inch thick. If the chops have become too long, you might need to cut each piece in half, because you don't want too much meat overlapping when you roll up the pieces.

4] Divide the bacon stuffing between the pork and spread it out in a thin, even layer. Roll up each pork piece from the short end, leaving just a little overlap of meat at the seam. Wrap 1 slice of the reserved bacon around each roll in a single layer, then tie with 2 pieces of string or carefully secure with wooden toothpicks. Season with pepper.

5] Heat the oil in a large skillet over medium heat. When the oil is shimmering, add the rolls and cook, turning regularly, 12 to 15 minutes until brown all over. Warm the tomato puree and spoon it over and around the rolls before serving with boiled fingerling potatoes and a green salad.

JOHNNIE'S TIP

The rolls can also be barbecued. Thread them onto wooden skewers that have been soaked in warm water 30 minutes. Brush the rolls with a little oil before seasoning, then barbecue 10 to 12 minutes, turning them regularly, until brown all over.

4 ounces sliced pancetta or thin smoked
   bacon slices

1 cup frozen peas

5 cups chicken stock

1 bay leaf

4 black peppercorns

4 tablespoons unsalted butter

3 shallots, very finely chopped

1/2 celery stalk, strings removed and
   minced

1 1/2 cups risotto rice, such as Arborio

1/2 cup dry white wine, at room temperature

4 tablespoons freshly shredded Grana Padano
   or Parmesan cheese, plus extra to serve

1 handful pea shoots (optional)

salt and freshly ground black pepper

SERVES 4 | **PREPARATION TIME** 15 minutes | **COOKING TIME** 40 minutes

PANCETTA & PEA RISOTTO

Sweet peas and salty pancetta complement each other well, especially against the backdrop of a creamy risotto. The shallots and celery should be cut very small, as tiny as the grains of rice, so they literally "melt" into the risotto.

1] Preheat the broiler to high. Broil the pancetta 3 to 4 minutes, turning once, until crisp, then transfer to a plate lined with paper towels. Reserve 4 slices of the pancetta (or 2 slices of bacon, if using) and break the remainder into small pieces, then leave to one side.

2] Put the peas in a colander and pour over just-boiled water. Leave to one side to drain.

3] Put the stock, bay leaf and peppercorns in a saucepan and warm over low heat until barely simmering. Melt 3 tablespoons of the butter in a large, heavy-bottomed saucepan over medium heat. Add the shallots and celery and cook about 8 minutes, stirring, until soft.

4] Add the rice and cook 3 to 4 minutes, stirring, until the grains looks slightly translucent around the edges. Pour in the wine and boil, stirring, until it has been absorbed.

5] Add a small ladleful of the stock and simmer, stirring continuously, until it is absorbed. Continue adding ladlefuls of stock, stirring after each addition, until the rice is tender but still has a slight "bite" to it; this should take 17 to 20 minutes and you might not need all the stock.

6] Gently stir in the drained peas, then remove the risotto from the heat and stir in the remaining butter, Grana Padano and pancetta pieces. Season to taste with salt and pepper and add a little extra stock if needed—the rice should be soft but still hold its shape. Serve the risotto topped with pieces of the reserved crisp pancetta and a few pea shoots, if using. Sprinkle extra Grana Padano over.

5 ounces sliced prosciutto, preferably prosciutto di Parma

about 2½ cups dry white wine

1 bay leaf

1 star anise

6 black peppercorns

9 ounces asparagus, trimmed

5 tablespoons unsalted butter

2 shallots, very finely chopped

½ celery stalk, strings removed and minced

1½ cups risotto rice, such as Arborio

1 tablespoon drained small capers

1¼ cups freshly shredded Grana Padano cheese, plus extra to serve

salt and freshly ground black pepper

SERVES 4 | PREPARATION TIME 15 minutes | COOKING TIME 40 minutes

PROSCIUTTO & ASPARAGUS RISOTTO

If asparagus is out of season, please avoid force grown or any other form and use calabrese, long-stem or purple-sprouting broccoli instead.

1] Put the prosciutto into a large, dry skillet over low heat. Cook 3 to 4 minutes, turning once, until crisp. Reserve 4 slices of the prosciutto and break the remainder into small pieces, then leave to one side.

2] Put the wine in a medium-sized saucepan with the bay leaf, star anise and peppercorns. Add 2½ cups water and bring to a boil. Turn down the heat to very low and keep the wine mixture warm.

3] Cut off the tips of the asparagus and set them aside. Cut the stalks into very fine dice. Melt 4 tablespoons of the butter in a large saucepan and add the shallots, celery and diced asparagus stalks. Cook very gently 10 minutes until the vegetables are soft.

4] Add the rice and cook 3 to 4 minutes, stirring, until the grains are slightly translucent around the edges. Add a small ladleful of the wine mixture and simmer, stirring continuously, until the liquid is absorbed. Continue adding ladlefuls of the wine mixture, stirring, until the rice is tender but still has a slight bite to it; this should take 17 to 20 minutes and you might not need all of the wine mixture. Remove the risotto from the heat and let it stand, covered, 2 minutes.

5] Meanwhile, cook the asparagus tips in boiling salted water 2 minutes until just tender.

6] Stir the remaining butter into the risotto with the capers and Grana Padano. Fold in the prosciutto pieces. Season with salt and pepper, to taste, and add a little extra liquid, if needed—the rice should be soft but still hold its shape. Serve the risotto topped with the asparagus tips, reserved prosciutto and sprinkled with extra Grana Padano.

1 tablespoon olive oil

1 onion, finely chopped

3 garlic cloves, crushed

1¼ cups Puy lentils, rinsed

½ cup dry white wine

1½ cups vegetable stock

1 long rosemary sprig, needles finely chopped

1 bay leaf

a pinch red pepper flakes

2 tablespoons vegetable oil

1 pound spicy link sausages, about 8 in total, such as Italian-style sausages or fresh chorizo sausages

1 handful flat-leaf parsley leaves, chopped

salt and freshly ground black pepper

crusty bread and arugula salad, to serve

SERVES 4 | **PREPARATION TIME** 10 minutes | **COOKING TIME** 45 minutes

SPICY SAUSAGE WITH LENTILS

Spicy sausages pair very well with the nutty, earthy flavor of Puy lentils to give a hearty, warming dish. Any leftovers are also good tossed with a little olive oil and lemon juice to make a lunchtime salad. Remember that good-quality sausages are a must.

1] Put the olive oil in a large saucepan over low heat. Add the onion and garlic and cook 8 to 10 minutes, stirring occasionally, until soft. Add the lentils, white wine, stock, rosemary, bay leaf and red pepper flakes. Increase the heat and bring the liquid to a boil. Boil the lentils 5 minutes, then turn down the heat, cover the pan and simmer 20 to 25 minutes until the liquid is absorbed and the lentils are tender.

2] Meanwhile, put the vegetable oil in a large skillet over medium heat. When the oil is shimmering, add the sausages and cook 15 minutes, turning regularly, until brown all over and cooked through. Leave the pan to one side until the lentils are ready.

3] Uncover the lentils and season with salt and pepper. Tip the lentils into the pan with the sausages and stir to combine. Warm over low heat 2 minutes, then remove the pan from the heat and scatter the parsley over. Serve with crusty bread and an arugula salad.

CURED, DRIED, PRESERVED & SMOKED

1 pound 2 ounces pork tenderloin, fat and silverskin membrane trimmed, cut into 8 equal pieces

16 slices prosciutto, preferably prosciutto di Parma

8 sage leaves

4 tablespoons unsalted butter

1 teaspoon vegetable oil

2 tablespoons dry white wine

1 tablespoon drained small capers

freshly ground black pepper

1 recipe quantity Green Beans with Garlic & Almonds (see page 218) or other green vegetable, such as peas, to serve

SERVES 4 | **PREPARATION TIME** 20 minutes | **COOKING TIME** 15 minutes

PORK SALTIMBOCCA

This variation on the veal classic is one of my favorite dishes, and it's simple, quick and very tasty.

1] Preheat the oven to 150°F. Put the pork pieces on a large cutting board, then cover with plastic wrap and beat with a meat mallet or rolling pin until 1/16 inch thick. Season each piece with a little pepper.

2] Lay 2 slices of prosciutto, slightly overlapping, on a clean cutting board or large plate and put a sage leaf in the middle. Sit a piece of pork on top. Wrap the prosciutto around the pork to make a package; the prosciutto should stick to itself, but you can secure it with a wooden toothpick, if necessary. Repeat to make 8 packages in total.

3] Heat the butter and oil in a large skillet over medium-high heat. When the butter is foaming, add the pork packages and cook 2 to 3 minutes on each side until the ham is crisp. You might need to cook them in two batches. Transfer the saltimbocca to the oven to keep warm.

4] Add the wine to the pan. Let it bubble 1 minute, then remove the pan from the heat and stir in the capers. Spoon the sauce and capers over the saltimbocca and serve with the green beans with garlic and almonds or other green vegetable.

¼ ounce dried porcini mushrooms

2 tablespoons unsalted butter

2 shallots, minced

1 garlic clove, crushed

3 cups thinly sliced cremini mushrooms

2 thyme sprigs, leaves removed

4 tablespoons Marsala

½ cup good-quality black olives, pitted and finely chopped

1 pound 2 ounces pork tenderloin, fat and silverskin membrane trimmed

6 to 10 thin smoked bacon slices

2 tablespoons vegetable oil

salt and freshly ground black pepper

1 recipe quantity Savoy Cabbage with Lardons (see page 219), boiled fingerling potatoes and lemon wedges, to serve

SERVES 4 | **PREPARATION TIME** 40 minutes, plus soaking | **COOKING TIME** 45 minutes

BACON-WRAPPED TENDERLOIN WITH MUSHROOM STUFFING

1] Put the porcini in a bowl and cover with just-boiled water. Leave to soak 30 minutes until soft. Strain, reserving the soaking liquid, and roughly chop the mushrooms.

2] Melt the butter in a large skillet over low heat. Add the shallots and garlic and cook 8 to 10 minutes until soft. Turn up the heat to medium-high, add the cremini mushrooms and thyme and cook about 10 minutes, stirring frequently, until the mushrooms are soft.

3] Add the porcini and cook 1 minute, then pour in the Marsala and mushroom soaking liquid and bring to a boil. Cook until the liquid evaporates, but the stuffing is still moist. Remove the pan from the heat, stir in the olives and season with salt and pepper to taste. Leave to cool slightly.

4] Make a horizontal cut along the middle of the pork, not quite slicing it all the way through. Open out the tenderloin like a book, cover with plastic wrap and beat with a meat mallet or rolling pin until the meat is ⅛ inch thick; try to keep the meat in a rectangular shape. Season with salt and pepper.

5] Lay the bacon slices vertically on a sheet of waxed paper, slightly overlapping them; you need to make a bed of bacon slightly longer than the tenderloin. Spread the mushroom filling down one side of the tenderloin and fold it over to encase the filling. Lay the tenderloin horizontally on top of the bacon and, using the paper to help you, roll the bacon around the tenderloin. It is a good idea to tie it with string to secure.

6] Preheat the oven to 400°F. Heat the oil in a large skillet over medium heat. Brown the pork 10 minutes, turning until golden all over. Transfer to a roasting pan and roast 12 minutes. Remove from the oven, and leave the pork to rest 10 minutes, then cut into 8 slices. Serve with the Savoy cabbage with lardons, potatoes and lemon wedges.

"SHOW ME HOW" TO WRAP THE TENDERLOIN

CHAPTER 3

SPICY & AROMATIC

Pork and spices were almost made for each other. The mild flavor of pork is a great canvas for spices—in fact, the meat benefits from the extra flavor.

It might come as little surprise pork is one of Asia's favorite meats, and chili-hot dishes, such as Pork Sichuan Noodles and Korean-Style Fiery Pork show how perfect pork is for Asian-style cooking. But it's not all about heat, so for a milder, but spicy, option, try the sweet-savory tang of Teriyaki Pork Skewers with Pickled Vegetables or Pork Dim Sum, which are both fun to make and eat.

Asian cooking doesn't have a monopoly on superbly spiced dishes, and there is plenty of inspiration in this chapter from Latin American countries, too, including South American-Style Pork Empanaditas, Hot Mexican Pork Burgers and Green Pork Chili Tacos. The Caribbean, too, is represented with a taste-bud-tingling Jerk Pork served with a cooling Mango Salsa, while there is also the ever-popular Spicy Pork Meatloaf.

Even the Europeans like to spice pork up. Look for the delicious Spanish Pork Skewers, or why not try making *pimentón*-spiked Fresh Chorizo Sausages? Whatever your mood or preference, there is a dish here to tempt you.

1 pound pork tenderloin, fat and silverskin membrane trimmed, cut into ¼-inch-thick slices

3 garlic cloves, crushed

1 lemongrass stalk, tough outer leaves removed, minced

3 tablespoons fish sauce

3 tablespoons soft light brown sugar

vegetable oil, for greasing

1 or 2 baguettes, cut into 4 pieces, each about 6 inches long

scant ½ cup mayonnaise

2 fresh red chilies, seeded and thinly sliced

1 large handful cilantro leaves

½ cucumber, seeded and cut into matchsticks

PICKLED VEGETABLES

1 carrot, cut into matchsticks

4½-inch piece daikon (mooli), peeled and cut into matchsticks

½ teaspoon salt

⅔ cup rice wine vinegar

4 tablespoons sugar

SERVES 4 | **PREPARATION TIME** 45 minutes, plus marinating | **COOKING TIME** 15 minutes

VIETNAMESE BAGUETTE

Called *Banh mi* in Vietnam, this is a sandwich that is usually filled with pork and pickled vegetables. I like to use a marinated tenderloin.

1] To make the pickled vegetables, put the carrot and daikon in a colander and toss with the salt; leave to one side 20 minutes until soft, then rinse and pat dry with paper towels. Mix together the vinegar, sugar and ½ cup warm water in a nonmetallic bowl until the sugar dissolves. Add the vegetables and leave to marinate 1 hour, or refrigerate until needed. (The vegetables will keep in the refrigerator up to 1 week.)

2] Meanwhile, cover the pork slices with plastic wrap, then beat with a meat mallet or rolling pin until about ⅛ inch thick.

3] Mix together the garlic, lemongrass, fish sauce and soft light brown sugar in a large bowl. Add the pork and turn to coat, then leave to marinate 30 minutes.

4] Heat a grill pan or large skillet over high heat until it is smoking hot. Brush with a little vegetable oil, then cook the marinated pork 2 to 3 minutes on each side. Don't overcrowd the pan, and you might need to cook the pork in batches. Transfer the cooked meat to a plate and leave to cool slightly.

5] Cut each portion of baguette in half lengthwise and hollow out the top section slightly to make room for the filling. Spread a little mayonnaise over the bottom and scatter the chilies over. Sit the pork slices on top, then add the cilantro and cucumber. Drain the vegetables and spoon them on top, sandwich everything together and serve.

4 cups vegetable stock

4 fresh red Thai or serrano chilies, roughly chopped

3 garlic cloves, thinly sliced

3 lemongrass stalks, tough outer leaves removed, roughly chopped

1-inch piece gingerroot, thinly sliced (no need to peel)

10 cilantro sprigs

2 kaffir lime leaves, or 3 long strips pared lime peel

3 ounces dry vermicelli rice noodles

½ teaspoon fish sauce

juice of ½ lime

1 tablespoon soft light brown sugar

10 ounces boneless pork loin chops, fat trimmed, cut into ⅛-inch cubes

3 ounces small oriental mushrooms, such as enoki or shimenji

5 ounces shelled cooked salad shrimp

fish sauce, thinly sliced fresh Thai chilies, lime wedges and 1 handful each cilantro leaves and Thai basil leaves (optional), to serve

SERVES 4 | PREPARATION TIME 25 minutes | COOKING TIME 40 minutes

HOT & SOUR NOODLE SOUP WITH PORK

I like to serve my hot-and-sour soup truly Thai-style, with each person helping themselves to extra fish sauce, chopped chilies, lime juice and cilantro, according to their own taste. Top each serving with a few Thai basil leaves, too, if available.

1] Put the vegetable stock in a large saucepan with the chilies, garlic, lemongrass, ginger, cilantro sprigs and kaffir lime leaves. Add 1 cup water. Bring to a boil over high heat, then turn down the heat to low and simmer 30 minutes.

2] Meanwhile, put the noodles into a large bowl and cover with warm water. Leave to soak 20 minutes until the noodles are just soft, then drain and leave to one side.

3] Strain the aromatic stock into a clean saucepan and stir in the fish sauce, lime juice and sugar. Bring the stock to a boil over high heat. Turn down the heat to low and add the pork, mushrooms and drained noodles. Simmer 2 to 3 minutes until the mushrooms are soft, then add the shrimp and cook 1 minute longer until they are warmed through.

4] Serve the soup, helping yourself to the extra fish sauce, chilies, lime wedges, cilantro and basil, if using.

1 tablespoon vegetable oil, plus extra
  for deep-frying

½ small onion, finely chopped

½ red bell pepper, seeded and finely diced

1 garlic clove, crushed

½ teaspoon ground cumin

½ teaspoon paprika

½ teaspoon cayenne pepper

7 ounces ground pork

3 tablespoons white wine or dry sherry

2 tablespoons raisins, finely chopped

6 pimento-stuffed green olives, finely chopped

salt and freshly ground black pepper

DOUGH

2½ cups all-purpose flour, plus extra
  for dusting

2 teaspoons baking powder

½ teaspoon salt

3 tablespoons vegetable shortening

½ cup milk

1 egg

SERVES 4 to 8 (makes 16) | PREPARATION TIME 45 minutes, plus cooling and chilling | COOKING TIME 45 minutes

SOUTH AMERICAN-STYLE PORK EMPANADITAS

These are wonderful for a picnic, dipped into a sweet-and-spicy sauce or mayonnaise.

1] Put the 1 tablespoon of oil in a large skillet over medium heat. Add the onion, pepper and garlic and cook 8 to 10 minutes until soft. Add the cumin, paprika and cayenne and cook 2 minutes, then transfer to a bowl. Turn up the heat to high.

2] Add the ground pork and cook, breaking it up with a spoon, 6 to 8 minutes until brown. Return the onion mixture to the pan, add the wine and 3 tablespoons water. Bring to a boil and cook 4 to 5 minutes until the liquid evaporates. Remove the pan from the heat and stir in the raisins and olives. Season and leave to one side to cool completely.

3] To make the dough, sift the flour, baking powder and salt into a large bowl. Cut the shortening into the flour until you can no longer see any lumps of fat. Whisk together the milk and egg and add to the flour mixture, a little at a time, to make a soft dough. Form the dough into a disk, wrap in plastic wrap and put in the refrigerator 1 hour.

4] Dust a work surface with flour, then roll out the dough and cut out 16 circles, roughly 4 inches in diameter. Put 1 heaped tablespoon of the filling on one side of a circle of dough. Dampen the edge of the dough with water, then fold it over to make a half-moon shape and crimp the edge with your fingers to seal. Repeat to make 16 in total.

5] Pour enough oil into a large saucepan to fill by one-third and heat to 350°. Fry the empanaditas for 4 minutes, turning occasionally, until golden. You will need to cook them in batches and bring the oil back to 350°F before adding a new batch. Transfer the empanaditas to a plate lined with paper towels and cool slightly before serving.

"SHOW ME HOW" TO FILL AND FRY THE EMPANADITAS

6 ounces boneless pork loin chop, fat trimmed, cut into cubes

4 ounces shelled cooked salad shrimp, patted dry

8 canned water chestnuts, drained and roughly chopped

6 scallions, finely chopped

1½-inch piece gingerroot, peeled and grated

1½ tablespoons oyster sauce

2 teaspoons soy sauce

1½ teaspoons sugar

28 won ton skins

chives, to serve

DIPPING SAUCE

4 tablespoons soy sauce

2 tablespoons rice wine vinegar

4 tablespoons soft light brown sugar

2 teaspoons toasted sesame oil

2 small scallions, thinly sliced

½ fresh red chili, seeded and diced

SERVES 4 (makes about 28) | **PREPARATION TIME** 40 minutes | **COOKING TIME** 25 minutes

PORK DIM SUM

These steamed dim sum dumplings resemble moneybags. Serve them as an appetizer, followed by a stir-fry and some rice. Sweet chili sauce is a good alternative to the dipping sauce.

1] Finely chop the pork in a food processor 1 to 2 minutes. Add the shrimp and pulse 6 to 8 times until chopped, then add the water chestnuts and scallions and pulse 4 to 6 times until combined. Transfer to a bowl and stir in the ginger, oyster and soy sauces and sugar.

2] Lay a won ton skin on a cutting board. Put a slightly heaped teaspoonful of the pork mixture in the middle and brush around the filling with water. Bring the corners of the won ton skin together, then squeeze and twist the top to seal and to make a "moneybag." Transfer to a baking sheet lined with plastic wrap and keep covered with more plastic wrap to prevent it drying out. Keep the unused won ton skins covered as well. Repeat with the remaining won ton skins and pork mixture until they are all used.

3] Line a large bamboo steamer with parchment paper. Put the dumplings in the steamer, making sure they don't touch each other, cover and steam over a wok or saucepan of boiling water 6 to 8 minutes. You might need to cook the dumplings in a tiered steamer or in batches.

4] To make the dipping sauce, mix together the soy sauce, vinegar, sugar and sesame oil with 4 tablespoons water. Divide into 4 small dipping bowls and scatter a little scallion and chili on top.

5] Scatter a few chives over the dim sum and serve with the dipping sauce.

"SHOW ME HOW" TO FILL AND FORM THE DIM SUM

1 pound 2 ounces ground pork

2 tablespoons Thai Green Curry Paste (see page 60)

1 bunch scallions, finely chopped

1 lemongrass stalk, tough outer leaves removed, minced

¾-inch piece gingerroot, peeled and grated

vegetable oil for frying

salt and freshly ground black pepper

20 crisp lettuce leaves, such as small romaine or iceberg

sweet chili sauce, 1 handful cilantro leaves and lime wedges, to serve

SERVES 4 (makes 20) | PREPARATION TIME 20 minutes | COOKING TIME 20 minutes

PORK & LEMONGRASS WRAPS

Fragrant, spiced pork wrapped in crisp lettuce leaves is a popular street snack in Thailand and all over Southeast Asia.

1] Put the pork into a large bowl and stir in the curry paste, scallions, lemongrass and ginger. Season with salt and pepper, then mix everything together thoroughly. You might like to check the seasoning by frying a teaspoonful of the mixture in a little vegetable oil and adding more salt and pepper, if needed.

2] Line a baking sheet with plastic wrap. Roll tablespoonfuls of the mixture into balls—you should have 20 in total—then put them on the baking sheet and flatten slightly to make patties, about ¾ inch thick.

3] Pour the vegetable oil into a large, deep skillet to a depth of ¼ inch. Put over medium-high heat and when the oil is shimmering, fry the patties 2 to 3 minutes on each side until crisp and just cooked though. Don't overcrowd the pan—you will probably need to cook the patties in batches.

4] Transfer the patties to a large plate lined with paper towels. Let everyone assemble their own wraps by taking a lettuce leaf and putting a patty in the middle. Add a little sweet chili sauce, a few cilantro leaves and a squeeze of lime before folding the lettuce around the patty.

¼ cup shelled unsalted peanuts

1 tablespoon vegetable oil

½-inch piece gingerroot, peeled and finely grated

2 garlic cloves, thinly sliced

4 scallions, finely chopped

9 ounces ground pork

1½ teaspoons fish sauce

1½ teaspoons soy sauce

2 teaspoons sugar

½ pineapple, skin and "eyes" removed

1 tablespoon lime juice, plus extra to taste

2 fresh red Thai or serrano chilies, thinly sliced

1 handful cilantro leaves

steamed jasmine rice, to serve (optional)

SERVES 4 | **PREPARATION TIME** 20 minutes | **COOKING TIME** 25 minutes

THAI PORK SALAD WITH PINEAPPLE

This recipe is based on a Thai salad called *Ma ho*, meaning "galloping horses." It is also popular as a canapé or appetizer. To serve either of these ways, cut thick cubes of pineapple and top each one with a spoonful of the pork mixture.

1] Toast the peanuts in a dry wok over medium heat 3 to 4 minutes, until browned. Transfer to a plate and leave to cool, then chop roughly.

2] Return the wok to the heat and add the oil. When the oil is shimmering, add the ginger, garlic and scallions and sizzle for a second, then add the pork and stir-fry 8–10 minutes until the pork is brown and crisp in places. Stir in the fish sauce, soy sauce and sugar and remove the wok from the heat. Leave the pork to cool 10 minutes until it reaches room temperature.

3] Cut the pineapple in half lengthwise and cut away and discard the core. Slice the pineapple thinly and spread the slices out on a plate. Stir the chopped peanuts and lime juice into the pork mixture, adding a little more lime, if you like, then spoon the pork over the pineapple.

4] Scatter the chilies and cilantro leaves over the pork and serve immediately. You can serve this as a first course or with sticky jasmine rice as a main course.

SPICY & AROMATIC

3 ounces dry rice vermicelli noodles

3 tablespoons fish sauce

3 tablespoons lime juice

2 tablespoons soft light brown sugar

4 boneless pork loin chops, each about
6 ounces, fat trimmed

4 fresh green Thai or serrano chilies, thinly
sliced

1/3 cup shelled unsalted peanuts

1 tablespoon vegetable oil

1 cucumber, seeded and cut into matchsticks

1 large carrot, cut into matchsticks

10 radishes, thinly sliced

1/2 red bell pepper, seeded and thinly sliced

2 tomatoes, seeded and thinly sliced

2 handfuls bean sprouts

1 large handful mint leaves

1 large handful cilantro leaves

SERVES 4 | **PREPARATION TIME** 40 minutes, plus soaking and chilling (optional) | **COOKING TIME** 20 minutes

VIETNAMESE PORK SALAD

Pork is probably the most popular meat in Vietnam and it is prepared in a variety of ways. Quickly fried until golden and served as part of a summery noodle salad, as here, is one of the best.

1] Put the noodles in a large bowl and cover with just-boiled water. Leave to one side 20 minutes until the noodles are soft, then drain, rinse with cold water and drain again. Chill the noodles 4 hours before using, if possible.

2] Whisk together the fish sauce, lime juice and sugar until the sugar dissolves. Rub 1 tablespoon of the mixture into the pork chops and leave them to stand 10 minutes. Add the chilies to the remaining fish sauce dressing and leave to one side.

3] Toast the peanuts 3 to 4 minutes in a large, dry skillet over medium heat. Transfer the peanuts to a plate to cool, then chop or crush roughly.

4] Add the oil to the pan and cook the pork chops about 3 minutes on each side until brown on the outside and just pink in the middle. Don't overcrowd the pan—you might need to cook in two batches. Cover the pork with foil and leave it to rest 5 minutes.

5] Put the drained noodles into a serving bowl with the cucumber, carrot, radishes, pepper, tomatoes, bean sprouts, mint and cilantro. Add the dressing and toss together. Slice the pork chops thinly. Serve the noodle salad topped with the pork strips and peanuts.

1 pound boneless pork loin chops, fat trimmed, cut into ½-inch cubes

¼ cucumber, seeded and cubed

8 small scallions, halved

steamed jasmine rice, to serve (optional)

MARINADE

4 tablespoons coconut milk

1 tablespoon soy sauce

1 tablespoon soft light brown sugar

1 tablespoon vegetable oil

1 lemongrass stalk, tough outer leaves removed, minced

6 cardamom pods, seeds crushed and pods discarded

½-inch piece gingerroot, peeled and grated

1 teaspoon garam masala

½ teaspoon turmeric

1 garlic clove, crushed

freshly ground black pepper

SATAY SAUCE

1 tablespoon vegetable oil

2 shallots, minced

½ teaspoon garam masala

¼-inch piece gingerroot, peeled and grated

1 fresh red chili, seeded and finely chopped

4 tablespoons unsweetened shredded coconut

5 tablespoons coconut milk

2 teaspoons soy sauce

2 teaspoons lime juice

1 teaspoon soft light brown sugar

SERVES 4 (makes 16) | **PREPARATION TIME** 30 minutes, plus overnight marinating | **COOKING TIME** 15 minutes

MAURITIAN PORK SATAY

Thai pork satay with peanut sauce is familiar to most people, yet in Mauritius they make a creamy coconut version that is slightly less fiery, but still aromatic and delicious.

1] Put the pork into a nonmetallic bowl. Mix together the marinade ingredients with a generous grinding of pepper, then pour it over the pork and toss to coat. Cover and marinate in the refrigerator 8 hours, or overnight.

2] Meanwhile, to make the satay sauce, put the oil in a saucepan over medium heat. Add the shallots and fry, stirring occasionally, 5 to 6 minutes until soft. Add the garam masala and ginger and fry 1 minute longer, then remove the pan from the heat and leave to cool. Stir in the remaining ingredients and refrigerate until needed. Thirty minutes before you are ready to cook, soak 16 wooden skewers in warm water to prevent them burning.

3] Preheat the broiler to high and line the broiler pan with foil. Thread pork cubes onto the skewers, then broil 3 to 4 minutes on each side until slightly charred and just cooked.

4] Put the cucumber and scallions in the middle of a serving platter and arrange the skewers around the edge. Give the satay sauce a stir and divide it into 4 small bowls. Serve the satay so each person can add a little cucumber and scallion to their skewers, then dip them in the sauce to eat. Serve with jasmine rice, if you like.

1 pound 9 ounces boneless pork loin chops, fat trimmed, cut into ½-inch cubes

½ onion, minced

2 garlic cloves, crushed

2 tablespoons olive oil

1½ teaspoons hot smoked paprika

½ teaspoon ground cumin

½ teaspoon ground coriander

½ teaspoon dried oregano

¼ teaspoon black pepper

salt

crusty bread and lemon wedges, to serve

SERVES 4 (makes 16) | **PREPARATION TIME** 30 minutes, plus overnight marinating | **COOKING TIME** 10 minutes

SPANISH PORK SKEWERS

Pinchos morunos, meaning "Moorish skewers," is a popular tapas dish offered in bars all over Spain. It can be served as part of a tapas platter with thinly sliced Hot-Smoked Pork Tenderloin (see page 82), small bowls of Chorizo Rancheros, without the eggs (see page 74) and thinly sliced manchego cheese. Fantastic!

1] Put the pork into a bowl and scatter the onion over. Mix together the garlic, oil, paprika, cumin, coriander, oregano and pepper. Spoon it over the pork and onion, then turn until coated. Cover and leave to marinate in the refrigerator 8 hours, or overnight.

2] Meanwhile, about 30 minutes before cooking, soak 16 wooden skewers in warm water to prevent them burning.

3] Preheat the broiler to high and line the broiler pan with foil. Remove the pork from the marinade and thread the cubes of pork onto the skewers. Brush with a little of the marinade left in the bowl and season each skewer with a little salt. Broil 3 to 4 minutes on each side until the pork is slightly charred and just cooked through.

4] Serve the skewers hot or at room temperature with crusty bread and lemon wedges.

4 boneless pork loin chops, about
1 pound 5 ounces total weight

TERIYAKI SAUCE
½ cup mirin
½ cup soy sauce
4 tablespoons sake or dry sherry
3 tablespoons soft light brown sugar

PICKLED VEGETABLES
½ cup rice vinegar
1½ tablespoons sugar
¼ teaspoon salt
1 small piece kombu seaweed (optional)
½ cucumber, peeled, seeded and cut
into matchsticks
2 carrots, cut into matchsticks

SERVES 4 | **PREPARATION TIME** 2½ hours | **COOKING TIME** 10 minutes

TERIYAKI PORK SKEWERS WITH PICKLED VEGETABLES

1] To make the pickled vegetables, mix together the vinegar, sugar, salt and kombu, if using, in a large nonmetallic bowl with 4 tablespoons just-boiled water. Add the cucumber and carrots and toss to coat them in the liquid, then leave to one side 1 to 2 hours.

2] Meanwhile, to make the sauce, put the mirin, soy sauce, sake and sugar in a medium-sized saucepan over high heat. Bring to a boil, then turn down the heat and simmer 20 minutes until it reduces by half. Leave to one side 1 hour to cool.

3] Cover the pork with plastic wrap and beat with a meat mallet or rolling pin until ¼ inch thick. Cut each chop into 3 long strips and transfer to a bowl. Pour the teriyaki sauce over, reserving 4 tablespoons to serve, and toss until coated. Leave to marinate 30 minutes, but not much longer, because the pork can become tough and dry if left for too long. Stir the pork every 10 minutes while it is marinating.

4] Meanwhile, preheat the broiler to high and line the broiler pan with foil. Remove the pork from the teriyaki sauce and thread it onto long metal skewers. Brush the pork with some of the sauce and broil 1 minute. Brush with more sauce and broil 2 minutes longer, then turn the skewers over and brush again. Broil 1 minute, brush with sauce a final time and broil a final 2 minutes until just cooked.

5] Drain the pickled vegetables and remove the kombu, if used. Serve the teriyaki pork skewers with the reserved sauce for drizzling over the top and the pickled vegetables.

12 ounces boneless pork loin chops,
  fat trimmed

7 teaspoons soy sauce

1 tablespoon Chinese cooking wine
  or dry sherry

2 teaspoons toasted sesame oil

1 teaspoon sugar

4 tablespoons vegetable oil

2 fresh red chilies, seeded and thinly sliced

3 garlic cloves, 2 thinly sliced and 1 crushed

1 handful parsley leaves, chopped

4 eggs

1-inch piece gingerroot, peeled and grated

6 scallions, thinly sliced

4 ounces shiitake mushrooms, thinly sliced

1 handful bean sprouts

1¾ cups drained canned bamboo shoots, cut
  into matchsticks

20 Mandarin or Chinese pancakes

about 6 tablespoons hoisin sauce

SERVES 4 | **PREPARATION TIME** 30 minutes | **COOKING TIME** 20 minutes

STIR-FRIED PORK WITH PANCAKES

1] Cover the pork with plastic wrap, then beat with a meat mallet or rolling pin until ⅛ inch thick. Cut the pork into finger-size pieces and transfer to a bowl. Add 2 tablespoons of the soy sauce, the Chinese cooking wine, sesame oil and sugar. Mix together until the pork is coated and leave to one side.

2] Heat 1 tablespoon of the vegetable oil in a large wok over medium-high heat and stir-fry the chilies, sliced garlic and parsley 1 minute until starting to color and turn crisp. Drain on paper towels and leave to one side.

3] To make the omelet, whisk the eggs with the remaining 1 teaspoon soy sauce and 1 tablespoon cold water. Put 1 tablespoon of the remaining vegetable oil in the wok or a large skillet over high heat. When the oil is shimmering, pour in the eggs, tilt the wok so they cover the bottom in an even layer and cook 1 to 2 minutes until golden on the bottom and slightly puffed up. Using a metal spatula, carefully flip the omelet over and cook 1 to 2 minutes longer until set. Cut into thin strips and leave to one side.

4] Heat the remaining vegetable oil in the wok and add the crushed garlic and ginger. Let them sizzle 30 seconds, then add the scallions and mushrooms and stir-fry 4 to 5 minutes until soft. Move the vegetables to one side of the wok, tip in the pork and any liquid left in the bowl and stir-fry 1 minute. Stir the vegetables into the pork and add the bean sprouts and bamboo shoots. Stir-fry 2 minutes longer, then stir in the omelet strips and remove the wok from the heat.

5] Heat the pancakes following the package directions. Scatter the reserved parsley mixture over the pork mixture. Let everyone serve themselves by spooning a pile of the pork in the middle of a pancake and then drizzling hoisin sauce over. Wrap the pancake around the filling and eat immediately.

1 pound pork tenderloin, fat and
   silverskin membrane trimmed, cut into
   $\frac{1}{16}$-inch-thick slices
2 garlic cloves, crushed
$\frac{3}{4}$-inch piece gingerroot, peeled and grated
2 tablespoons *gochujang* paste or hot
   chili paste

2 tablespoons soy sauce
2 tablespoons mirin
2 tablespoons soft light brown sugar
2 teaspoons sesame oil
vegetable oil, for greasing
boiled white rice, romaine lettuce leaves
   and kimchi (optional), to serve

SERVES 4 | **PREPARATION TIME** 15 minutes, plus marinating | **COOKING TIME** 15 minutes

KOREAN-STYLE FIERY PORK

The pork must be cut and then beaten into very thin slices and cooked over very high heat in this classic Korean dish, called *daeji bulgogi*. You will find *gochujang* (Korean hot pepper) paste in Asian grocery stores or online, but you can use any hot chili paste. Any leftovers are fantastic as part of a filling for the Vietnamese Baguette (see page 114).

1] Cover the pork slices with plastic wrap, then beat with a meat mallet or rolling pin until very thin, about $\frac{1}{16}$ inch thick.

2] Mix the garlic, ginger, *gochujang* paste, soy sauce, mirin, sugar and sesame oil together in a large bowl. Add the pork and toss to coat, then leave to marinate 30 minutes.

3] Heat a cast-iron, ridged grill pan or a large skillet over high heat until it is smoking hot. Brush with a little vegetable oil, then cook the marinated pork 1 to 2 minutes on each side until cooked through. You will need to do this in batches, pressing the slices of pork onto the ridges of the griddle with a pair of tongs to get the charred lines. Transfer the cooked pork to a warm serving dish and cover with foil while you cook the remaining pork.

4] Serve the pork with a boiled rice, lettuce and the kimchi by the side, if using. Alternatively, serve the pork wrapped in the lettuce leaves with the kimchi.

JOHNNIE'S TIP

It is important to trim the silverskin or white connective tissue surrounding the pork tenderloin, because it becomes very tough as it cooks. If the recipe calls for the tenderloin to be cooked whole, it looks better if the ends are trimmed first to neaten the appearance. The trimmed ends can be saved and stir-fried or beaten into medallions for another meal.

2 pieces pork tenderloin, each about 1 pound,
    fat and silverskin membrane trimmed

1 tablespoon coriander seeds

3 tablespoons vegetable oil

1 teaspoon sesame seeds

2 garlic cloves, thinly sliced

½-inch piece gingerroot, peeled and grated

1 fresh red chilli, seeded and thinly sliced

2 teaspoons toasted sesame oil

2 bok choy, quartered lengthwise

1 green bell pepper, seeded and thinly sliced

1¾ cups drained canned bamboo
    shoots, cut into matchsticks

1¼ cups bean sprouts

2 tablespoons hoisin sauce

2 teaspoons soy sauce

a pinch of sugar

juice of ½ lime

1 handful cilantro leaves

salt and freshly ground black pepper

steamed jasmine or basmati rice and
    lime wedges, to serve

SERVES 4 to 6 | **PREPARATION TIME** 30 minutes | **COOKING TIME** 30 minutes

CORIANDER-CRUSTED PORK

1] Trim the ends of the pieces of tenderloin to neaten them, if you like. Toast the coriander seeds in a dry skillet 4 minutes until they smell aromatic, then crush and mix with some salt and pepper. Scatter this mixture evenly over a baking sheet and roll each piece of pork in the coriander mixture to coat evenly.

2] Put 2 tablespoons of the oil in a large skillet over medium-high heat. When the oil is shimmering, add the tenderloins and cook 18 minutes, giving them a quarter turn every 2 minutes and turning down the heat slightly if the pork browns too quickly. Don't forget to brown the cut ends of the pieces for a minute or so as well. This should give you slightly pink meat, but it will still be nice and juicy. Transfer the pork to a plate, cover and leave to rest.

3] Toast the sesame seeds in a wok 2 to 3 minutes, then transfer to a plate and leave to one side. Put the remaining oil in the wok over high heat. Add the garlic, ginger and chili and stir-fry 1 minute, then add the sesame oil.

4] Add the bok choy and stir-fry 4 minutes until just starting to color. Move it to one side of the wok, add the green pepper and bamboo shoots and stir-fry 3 to 4 minutes until soft. Add the bean sprouts and stir-fry 1 minute longer, then remove the wok from the heat and toss all of the vegetables together with the hoisin sauce, soy sauce, sugar and lime juice.

5] Slice each piece of pork and sit the slices on top of the vegetables. Drizzle any juices that have collected on the plate while the pork was resting over. Scatter the coriander and sesame seeds on top and serve with rice and lime wedges.

"SHOW ME HOW" TO SPICE-COAT THE PORK

2 pieces pork tenderloin, each about 9 ounces,
   fat and silverskin membrane trimmed
4 tablespoons hoisin sauce, plus extra to serve
2 tablespoons turbinado sugar
1½ tablespoons soy sauce
1 tablespoon rice wine vinegar or dry sherry

1 tablespoon honey
½-inch piece gingerroot, peeled and grated
1 small bunch of chives, roughly chopped
steamed jasmine or basmati rice, and
   cucumber, seeded and cut into matchsticks,
   to serve

SERVES 4 | **PREPARATION TIME** 10 minutes, plus overnight marinating and resting |
COOKING TIME 30 minutes

CHINESE BARBECUE PORK [*pictured overleaf*]

Chinese barbecue pork, or *char siu*, is roasted at high heat until golden and sticky. It's
delicious served warm, but is equally good cold as a filling for the Vietnamese Baguette
(see page 114) or as part of the Pork with Egg-Fried Rice (see page 58).

1] Put the pork into a large, resealable plastic bag. Mix together the hoisin, sugar, soy sauce,
   rice wine vinegar, honey and ginger, then pour it over the pork to cover. Seal the bag,
   squeezing out as much air as possible, then put it in a shallow bowl in the refrigerator
   8 hours, or overnight.

2] Preheat the oven to 425°F. Place a wire rack over a roasting pan and pour about ½ inch
   water into the pan. Remove the pork from the marinade and set it on the rack. Brush
   generously with some of the marinade, then roast 15 minutes.

3] Reduce the oven temperature to 350°F. Brush the pork with more of the remaining
   marinade, then roast 15 minutes longer until dark and sticky on the outside and slightly
   pink in the middle.

4] Let the pork rest 10 minutes before cutting it into slices. Put the pork on top of the
   rice and scatter the chives over. Serve with cucumber and a little extra hoisin sauce
   drizzled over.

1 pound boneless pork loin chops, fat trimmed, cut into bite-size pieces

4 tablespoons cornstarch

4 tablespoons soy sauce

4 tablespoons rice wine or dry sherry

2/3 cup shelled unsalted peanuts

2 tablespoons vegetable oil

1/2 teaspoon red pepper flakes

2 fresh red chilies, seeded and thinly sliced

1 lemongrass stalk, tough outer leaves removed, minced

1-inch piece gingerroot, peeled and grated

4 garlic cloves, very thinly sliced

1 tablespoon rice wine vinegar

1 tablespoon sugar, plus extra to taste

4 scallions, thinly sliced

1 handful cilantro leaves

steamed jasmine rice, to serve

SERVES 4 | **PREPARATION TIME** 15 minutes, plus marinating | **COOKING TIME** 15 minutes

LEMONGRASS & GINGER STIR-FRY PORK

Stir-fried pork, *kung pao*-style, comes from the Sichuan Province in China, so it is full of bold flavors and very spicy—perfect for anyone who loves chilies, ginger and peanuts.

1] Put the pork into a large bowl and sprinkle the cornstarch over, then add the soy sauce and rice wine. Mix everything together and leave to marinate 30 minutes, then drain the pork, reserving the marinade. Add 1/2 cup water to the marinade.

2] Toast the peanuts in a dry wok or large skillet over medium heat 3 to 4 minutes. Transfer to a plate and leave to one side. Put the oil in the wok over high heat. When the oil is shimmering, add the red pepper flakes, chilies, lemongrass, ginger and garlic and sizzle 1 minute. Add the drained pork and stir-fry 4 to 5 minutes until just cooked.

3] Add the reserved marinade and bring to a boil, stirring, until the sauce thickens. Add a splash of extra water if it becomes too thick; the sauce should just cling to the meat.

4] Remove the wok from the heat and stir in the peanuts, vinegar and sugar. Taste and add a little extra sugar if you like; you should have a balance of sour and sweet. Scatter the scallions and cilantro over the top, and serve with jasmine rice.

10 ounces dry medium egg noodles

2 teaspoons sesame oil

1 pound 2 ounces ground pork

2 tablespoons soft light brown sugar

2 tablespoons oyster sauce

2 tablespoons vegetable oil

1 teaspoon Sichuan peppercorns, crushed

½ teaspoon red pepper flakes

1-inch piece gingerroot, peeled and grated

4 garlic cloves, thinly sliced

1 bunch scallions, thinly sliced

4 bok choy, thinly sliced

3 tablespoons soy sauce

1 handful cilantro leaves

lime wedges, to serve

SERVES 4 | **PREPARATION TIME** 20 minutes | **COOKING TIME** 25 minutes

PORK SICHUAN NOODLES

Also known as *dan dan* noodles, this stir-fry has a great combination of textures, plus a spicy kick from the Sichuan peppercorns.

1] Cook the noodles following the directions on the package. Drain and toss the noodles in the sesame oil, then leave to one side.

2] Heat a wok or a large skillet over high heat. Add the pork and stir-fry 8 to 10 minutes until it is brown and crisp in places. Stir in the sugar and oyster sauce, then transfer the pork mixture to a bowl.

3] Return the wok to the heat and add the oil. When the oil is shimmering, add the Sichuan peppercorns, red pepper flakes, ginger, garlic and scallions. Let them sizzle 1 minute, then add the bok choy and stir-fry 2 to 3 minutes until it wilts.

4] Return the pork to the wok, add the noodles and stir-fry 2 to 3 minutes longer until the noodles are heated through. Remove the wok from the heat and stir in the soy sauce. Scatter the cilantro over the top and serve with lime wedges for squeezing over.

12 ounces boneless pork loin chops,
  fat trimmed

3 tablespoons cornstarch

2/3 cup chicken stock

3 tablespoons oyster sauce

2 tablespoons soy sauce

2 tablespoons turbinado sugar

2 tablespoons vegetable oil

1-inch piece gingerroot, peeled and grated

2 garlic cloves, crushed

1 small onion, thinly sliced

4 ounces fresh shiitake mushrooms, tough
  stems removed, sliced

4 ounces enoki or shimenji mushrooms
  (or extra shiitake)

4 ounces snow peas

1½ cups bean sprouts

1 teaspoon sesame oil

1 can (8-oz.) water chestnuts, drained
  and sliced

4 scallions, thinly sliced

1 fresh red chili, seeded and thinly sliced

steamed jasmine rice, to serve

SERVES 4 | **PREPARATION TIME** 30 minutes | **COOKING TIME** 20 minutes

PORK & MUSHROOM STIR-FRY

To avoid overcooking the pork, I stir-fry it separately from the vegetables and add the sauce while the meat is still slightly pink. By the time the sauce has come to a boil, the meat is perfectly cooked.

1] Cover the pork with plastic wrap, then beat with a meat mallet or rolling pin until about 1/16 inch thick. Cut the pork into finger-size pieces and transfer to a bowl. Toss the pork in 2 tablespoons of the cornstarch and set aside. Mix the remaining cornstarch with the stock, oyster and soy sauces and sugar, then leave to one side.

2] Put 1 tablespoon of the oil in a wok or large skillet over high heat. When the oil is shimmering, add the ginger and garlic and sizzle 30 seconds. Add the onion and stir-fry 3 to 4 minutes until turning golden at the edges. Next, add the mushrooms and stir-fry 2 to 3 minutes until soft, then add the snow peas and stir-fry 2 minutes. Finally, add the bean sprouts and stir-fry 1 minute longer until they are slightly soft but still crisp. Transfer the vegetables to a large bowl.

3] Add the remaining oil to the wok and heat again until shimmering. Add the sesame oil and the pork, spread it out in the wok and cook 1 to 2 minutes until brown on the underside but still slightly pink on top. Return the vegetables to the wok with the stock mixture and water chestnuts and bring to a boil, stirring, then stir-fry about 30 seconds until the sauce thickens. Sprinkle with the scallions and chili and serve immediately with jasmine rice.

SPICY & AROMATIC

2 pieces pork tenderloin, each about 1 pound,
    fat and silverskin membrane trimmed
baked sweet potatoes, to serve

JERK PASTE
2 fresh Scotch Bonnet chilies, seeded and
    roughly chopped
2 garlic cloves, roughly chopped
2 tablespoons vegetable oil
1 tablespoon lime juice
1 teaspoon ground allspice
1 teaspoon soy sauce
1 teaspoon turbinado sugar

½-inch piece gingerroot, peeled and
    roughly chopped
¼ teaspoon ground black pepper
2 thyme sprigs, leaves removed

MANGO SALSA
1 large mango, peeled, seeded and diced
4 scallions, finely chopped
8 mint leaves, finely chopped
2 tablespoons lime juice
2 teaspoons olive oil
salt and freshly ground pepper

SERVES 4 to 6 | **PREPARATION TIME** 25 minutes, plus overnight marinating |
COOKING TIME 20 minutes

JERK PORK WITH MANGO SALSA

Jerk pork can be found all over Jamaica, from the most stylish restaurants to roadside stands. The jerk paste, with typical ingredients of allspice and Scotch Bonnet chilies, was probably originally used to preserve meat, but now it is popular for its spicy kick. If you want really hot jerk pork, then use three chilies instead of two.

1] Put the jerk paste ingredients into a blender or food processor. Blend everything to a paste, adding 1 tablespoon water, if necessary.

2] Using a small, sharp knife, poke holes into the pieces of pork to let the marinade penetrate slightly. Rub the jerk paste all over the pork, then wrap each piece tightly in plastic wrap and leave to marinate in the refrigerator 8 hours, or overnight.

3] Mix together all the salsa ingredients and season with salt and pepper, to taste. Refrigerate until needed.

4] Preheat the broiler to high. Unwrap the pork and broil 18 to 20 minutes, turning regularly, until the pork is a little charred on the outside but still slightly pink in the middle. Cover the pork with foil and leave to rest 10 minutes before slicing. Serve the pork with the mango salsa and baked sweet potatoes.

1 tablespoon vegetable oil
2 shallots, finely chopped
1 garlic clove, crushed
1 red chilli, seeded and finely chopped
a pinch red pepper flakes
1-inch piece gingerroot, peeled and grated
5 tablespoons apricot jam
2/3 cup tomato ketchup
1 1/2 tablespoons Worcestershire sauce
1 1/2 tablespoons apple cider vinegar
2 teaspoons Dijon mustard

4 bone-in pork chops, each about 7 ounces, fat trimmed
1 handful cilantro leaves
salt and freshly ground black pepper
baby leaf spinach salad, to serve

YELLOW RICE
1 cup basmati rice
1 teaspoon turmeric
1 cinnamon stick, about 4 inches
1 tablespoon unsalted butter

SERVES 4 | **PREPARATION TIME** 30 minutes, plus overnight marinating | **COOKING TIME** 35 minutes

SOUTH AFRICAN PORK CHOPS WITH YELLOW RICE

1] Put the oil in a medium-sized saucepan over medium heat. Fry the shallots, garlic, red pepper flakes and chilies, stirring, 5 to 6 minutes until the shallots are soft but not colored. Add the ginger and cook 1 minute. Remove the pan from the heat and stir in the jam, ketchup, Worcestershire sauce, vinegar and mustard. Leave to cool completely.

2] Put the pork chops in a nonmetallic dish and season with salt and pepper. Add the marinade and turn the chops until evenly coated. Cover and leave to marinate in the refrigerator 8 hours, or overnight.

3] Preheat the oven to 350°F. Line a baking sheet with parchment paper. Remove the chops from the marinade, shaking off any excess, and put them on the baking sheet. Reserve the marinade. Roast the chops 15 to 20 minutes until just cooked.

4] Meanwhile, make the yellow rice. Rinse the rice under cold running water until it runs clear. Transfer the rice to a medium-sized saucepan and add the turmeric, cinnamon stick and 1/2 teaspoon salt. Pour in 2 cups water and bring to a boil over medium heat, stirring occasionally. Turn down the heat to low, cover and cook the rice 10 minutes until the water is absorbed. Remove the pan from the heat and leave the rice to stand 10 minutes, then remove the cinnamon stick and stir in the butter with a fork, fluffing the rice up as you stir.

5] Transfer the reserved marinade to a small saucepan and add 2 tablespoons water. Bring to a boil over high heat, then turn down the heat and simmer 4 to 5 minutes until the sauce thickens. (Do not serve the marinade without boiling it first.)

6] Serve the rice topped with a chop and a spoonful of the warm marinade. Scatter the cilantro over the top and serve with a baby leaf spinach salad.

2 tablespoons vegetable oil

1 bunch scallions, thinly sliced

1 green bell pepper, seeded and finely diced

1 garlic clove, crushed

1/4 teaspoon ground cumin

1/4 teaspoon cayenne pepper

3 fresh green chilies, seeded and very finely diced

1 pound 2 ounces ground pork

2 tomatoes, seeded and diced

1 cup vegetable stock

salt and freshly ground black pepper

12 taco shells, sour cream, seeded and diced fresh green chilies, 1 large pitted, peeled and thinly sliced avocado, cilantro leaves, 1 cup shredded cheddar cheese and limes wedges, to serve

SERVES 4 | PREPARATION TIME 20 minutes | COOKING TIME 1½ hours

GREEN PORK CHILI TACOS

Green pork chili is slightly lighter than its tomato-based alternative, but it still makes a perfect filling for tacos, because it doesn't overpower the flavor of the accompaniments. You can also serve the chili with warm corn tortillas, instead of the tacos.

1] Put 1 tablespoon of the oil in a medium-sized Dutch oven or a heavy-bottomed saucepan over medium heat. Add the scallions and green pepper and cook 8 to 10 minutes until soft. Add the garlic, cumin, cayenne pepper and chilies and cook 2 minutes, stirring. Transfer to a bowl and leave to one side.

2] Heat the remaining oil in the Dutch oven and turn up the heat to high. Add the ground pork and cook, breaking it up with a wooden spoon, about 10 minutes until any liquid evaporates and the pork is brown. You might find it easier to cook the pork in two batches, because it can steam in its own juices if the pan is too crowded.

3] Return the pepper and onion mixture to the casserole and add the tomatoes and stock. Bring to a boil, stirring to dissolve any brown sediment around the edge of the pan, then turn down the heat to low and simmer, uncovered, about 1 hour until the liquid evaporates but the pork is still moist. Season with salt and pepper, to taste.

4] To serve, warm the tacos following the package directions. Sit the chili in the middle of the table and let everyone help themselves by piling the chili into the taco shells and topping them with the sour cream, green chilies, avocado, cilantro and cheese. A squeeze of lime adds the finishing touch.

2 tablespoons vegetable oil
1 onion, finely chopped
½ celery stalk, finely diced
½ carrot, finely diced
2 garlic cloves, crushed
2 teaspoons ancho chili powder
  or chili powder
½ teaspoon ground cumin
1 pound 2 ounces ground pork
⅔ cup red wine or chicken stock
½ teaspoon dried oregano

1 can (15-oz.) crushed tomatoes
¼ teaspoon sugar
1 cinnamon stick, about 4 inches
1 bay leaf
1 can (15-oz.) kidney beans, drained
¾ ounce good-quality dark chocolate
  (70% cocoa solids)
salt and freshly ground black pepper
sour cream, cilantro leaves, lime wedges and
  boiled jasmine or basmati rice, to serve

SERVES 4 | **PREPARATION TIME** 15 minutes | **COOKING TIME** 1 hour 30 minutes

MEXICAN CHILI

This chili has a hint of chocolate to take the flavor to another level.

1] Put 1 tablespoon of the oil in a medium-sized Dutch oven or a heavy-bottomed saucepan over low heat. Add the onion, celery, carrot and garlic and cook gently, stirring, about 10 minutes until translucent and soft. Add the chili powder and cumin, turn up the heat to medium and cook, stirring occasionally, 2 minutes. Transfer the vegetables to a bowl and leave to one side.

2] Heat the remaining oil in the casserole and turn up the heat to high. Add the ground pork and cook, breaking it up with a wooden spoon, about 10 minutes until any liquid evaporates and the pork is brown. You might find it easier to cook the pork in two batches, because it can steam in its own juices if the pan is too crowded. Add the wine to the pan and bring to a boil, stirring with a spoon to dissolve the brown bits around the edge of the pan, then bubble about 5 minutes until the liquid reduces by half.

3] Return the vegetables to the pan with the oregano, tomatoes, sugar, cinnamon and bay leaf. Bring to a boil, then turn down the heat to low, cover the pan and simmer 40 minutes. Uncover the pan, add the kidney beans and simmer 20 minutes longer until the sauce thickens.

4] Remove the cinnamon stick and bay leaf. Stir in the chocolate until it melts, then season with salt and pepper to taste. Top the chili with spoonfuls of sour cream, cilantro leaves and lime wedges for squeezing over. Serve with rice by the side.

SPICY & AROMATIC

2 tablespoons vegetable oil

1 onion, finely chopped

1 garlic clove, crushed

1 teaspoon red pepper flakes

3/4 teaspoon cayenne pepper

1/2 teaspoon chili powder

1/2 teaspoon fresh oregano leaves

1 fresh red chilli, seeded and diced

1 pound ground pork

4 sesame buns, split in half and toasted

4 large lettuce leaves

1 recipe quantity Chunky Fries (see page 215), to serve

TOMATO SALSA

4 tomatoes, skinned, seeded and chopped

4 scallions, thinly sliced

1 handful cilantro leaves, chopped

1 tablespoon lime juice

salt and freshly ground black pepper

LIME CREAM

4 tablespoons sour cream

finely grated zest of 1/2 lime

juice of 1 lime

SERVES 4 | **PREPARATION TIME** 20 minutes | **COOKING TIME** 20 minutes

HOT MEXICAN PORK BURGERS

You can choose how fiery you like these burgers, but remember that the salsa and lime cream will act as great heat "extinguishers."

1] To make the salsa, mix together all the ingredients in a nonmetallic bowl. Season with salt and pepper to taste and leave to one side. Mix together the ingredients for the lime cream in a small bowl and leave to one side.

2] Put 1 tablespoon of the oil in a small skillet over medium heat. Add the onion and cook 6 to 8 minutes until soft. Add the garlic, red pepper flakes, cayenne, chili powder and oregano and cook 2 minutes. Transfer the mixture to a bowl and leave to cool slightly.

3] Add the fresh chili and ground pork to the bowl and season with salt and pepper. Mix gently together and form into 4 burgers. Try not to squash the mixture too much, or the burgers will become too dense.

4] Put the remaining oil in a large skillet over medium heat. When the oil is shimmering, add the burgers and cook 1 minute, then turn down the heat slightly and cook 4 minutes until brown underneath. Flip the burgers and cook 3 to 4 minutes on the other side until just cooked through.

5] Serve the burgers in a sesame bun with lettuce and a spoonful each of salsa and lime cream. Serve with chunky fries on the side.

3 slices white bread, crusts removed, torn into small pieces

½ cup milk

1 tablespoon vegetable oil

1 onion, finely chopped

1 garlic clove, crushed

1 teaspoon fresh oregano leaves, roughly chopped, or ½ teaspoon dried oregano

⅔ cup tomato ketchup

3 tablespoons honey

2 teaspoons Worcestershire sauce

2 teaspoons good-quality balsamic vinegar

1 teaspoon soy sauce

½ teaspoon hot-pepper sauce, or to taste

scant ½ cup apple juice

1 pound ground pork

10 to 12 thin smoked bacon slices

salt and freshly ground black pepper

SERVES 4 | **PREPARATION TIME** 20 minutes, plus resting | **COOKING TIME** 50 minutes

SPICY PORK MEATLOAF

The meatloaf is wrapped in thinly sliced smoked bacon, which lends a delicious smoky flavor and also helps to retain the natural juiciness of the ground pork.

1] Preheat the oven to 350°F and line a baking sheet with parchment paper.

2] Put the bread in a bowl with the milk and leave to soak 15 minutes.

3] Meanwhile, put the oil in a small skillet over medium heat. Add the onion, garlic and oregano and cook 6 to 8 minutes, sirring, until the onion is soft. Transfer the onion mixture to a large bowl and leave to cool slightly.

4] Mix together the ketchup, honey, Worcestershire sauce, vinegar, soy sauce and hot-pepper sauce in a small saucepan. Set aside 6 tablespoons of the mixture. Add the apple juice to the pan and leave to one side.

5] Add the pork to the onion mixture in the bowl. Squeeze as much milk as possible out of the bread and add this to the bowl, along with 4 tablespoons of the reserved sauce. Season with salt and pepper.

6] Lay the bacon slices vertically on a sheet of parchment paper. Spoon the meatloaf mixture along one half of the bacon, moulding it into a log shape. Fold the bacon over the top of the meatloaf mixture and tuck it under, using the parchment paper to help you. Fold back the paper and put the loaf on the baking sheet. Bake for 20 minutes, then brush the top with the remaining 2 tablespoons of the reserved sauce and bake for a further 20 minutes. Leave to rest, loosely covered, for 20 minutes to firm up a little.

7] Put the sauce in the pan over high heat and bring to a boil, stirring. Bubble 1 minute until it thickens, then leave to cool slightly and add more hot pepper sauce if you like a sauce with extra kick. Serve the meatloaf in thick slices with a little sauce spooned over.

"SHOW ME HOW" TO MOLD AND WRAP THE MEATLOAF

2 tablespoons olive oil

1 onion, finely chopped

1 carrot, finely chopped

1 celery stalk, finely chopped

2 garlic cloves, crushed

scant 1 cup finely chopped cremini
mushrooms

2¼ pounds ground pork

½ teaspoon each ground cinnamon and
ground allspice

3 whole cloves

3 thyme sprigs

1 bay leaf

4 tablespoons Marsala

1¼ cups beef stock

½ cup fresh bread crumbs

1 egg, to glaze

salt and freshly ground black pepper

tomato ketchup, tomato relish or chili sauce,
boiled potatoes and green beans, to serve

PASTRY DOUGH

3¼ cups all-purpose flour

½ teaspoon salt

7 tablespoons chilled unsalted butter, diced

½ cup vegetable shortening, diced

1 egg, refrigerator cold

2 tablespoons chilled water

SERVES 4 to 6 | PREPARATION TIME 1 hour, plus chilling | COOKING TIME 2 hours

CHRISTMAS-SPICED CANADIAN PORK PIE

Cinnamon, cloves, allspice, ground pork and Marsala come together to make a cracking Christmas (or any other time) alternative pork pie.

1] To make the filling, heat the oil in a large sauté pan or a deep skillet over medium heat. Add the onion, carrot, celery and garlic and cook 8 to 10 minutes, stirring, until soft. Add the mushrooms and cook 10 minutes longer, stirring, until soft and any liquid that is released by the mushrooms evaporates. Transfer the vegetables to a bowl.

2] Return the pan to the heat. Add the ground pork and cook, breaking it up with a wooden spoon, 15 minutes until the pork is brown. Add the ground spices and cook 1 minute longer, then return the vegetables to the pan and add the cloves, thyme, bay leaf, Marsala and stock.

3] Bring to a boil, then turn down the heat, cover the pan and simmer 30 minutes. Remove the lid and simmer 10 to 15 minutes longer until there is only about 1 tablespoon liquid left in the pan. Remove the pan from the heat and pick out the cloves, bay leaf and thyme. Stir in the bread crumbs and season generously with salt and pepper. Leave the filling to cool completely.

4] Meanwhile, to make the dough, put the flour and salt in a food processor and pulse a couple of times to mix. Add the butter and shortening and process until the mixture looks like fine bread crumbs. Whisk together the egg and chilled water and add 4 tablespoons of the mixture to the food processor. Pulse 6 to 8 times to distribute the liquid, then switch off the food processor and press a few chunks of dough together with your fingers. If the lumps are dry, add another 1 tablespoon of the egg mixture and pulse again. If the lumps hold together, tip the mixture onto a work surface and gently bring it together to make a smooth dough. Wrap the dough in plastic wrap and chill 30 minutes.

5] To assemble the pie, divide the dough into two pieces, with one slightly larger than the other. Roll out the largest piece of dough into a circle and use to line a 9-inch pie dish. Spoon the cold filling into the dish. Roll out the remaining dough to a circle large enough to cover the pie. Dampen the edges of the dough with water, then lay the second piece of dough on top. Trim the excess dough and crimp the edges. Decorate the pie with the dough trimmings, if liked. Chill 30 minutes.

6] Preheat the oven to 400°F. To glaze the pie, whisk the egg with a pinch of salt, then brush it over the top. Cut a steam hole in the middle of the top crust and place the pie on a baking sheet. Bake 10 minutes, then reduce the oven temperature to 350°F and bake 30 to 35 minutes longer until the pastry is golden brown. Leave the pie to stand 30 minutes before serving with ketchup, potatoes and green beans.

HOW TO MAKE SAUSAGES

To be honest, store-bought link sausages can be a bit hit or miss and differ massively in quality. So, if you really want to be sure of the quality of your sausages, it is possible to make them at home without too much difficulty.

A sausage consists of a filling and a skin, called a casing. The casing can be a pig's intestines, usually called "natural casings," or made from collagen, which is stretched to make long tubes. Both are available online, and whichever one you go for tends to be a matter of personal preference and availability rather than anything else. You will need to soak the casings before use, and because natural casings are usually salted they might need a longer soaking in several changes of water.

The meaty filling does need some fat to stop it becoming dry while it cooks, and a ratio of roughly 1 part fat to 4 parts meat is regarded as a good one to work to. Fortunately, equal quantities of pork belly and shoulder usually gives about the right mix. If you are using ground pork, avoid a lean or low-fat version. If you want to grind your own pork, you will need a grinder, because food processors tend to make the mixture too fine. After this, fresh bread crumbs can be added to give the sausages a slightly softer texture, but the filler should be less than 10 percent of the total weight of the meat.

The fun part of making your own sausages is adding the flavorings, and here you can really let your own palate dictate: sage and allspice produce a traditional British "banger"; red wine and fennel seeds give sausages an Italian twist; chilies and spices add a Mexican or Spanish flavor, as in the classic chorizo sausage. Be generous with the salt and pepper, and remember to fry a small portion to taste and check the seasonings before you begin filling the casings.

The final stage of sausage making is the filling and it's usually done with a sausage maker and/or a long tube that attaches to the grinder, but it is possible to use a large pastry bag, a wide tip and a willing helper to stuff the casings. Rinse the casing and tie a knot in one end. Ease the other end of the casing over the tip, ruching as much of it over the tip as you can. Push the sausage mixture into the casing in a slow, steady stream and keep going until the casing is almost full, then tie the open end. Twist the sausage at intervals to form links.

Once the casings have been filled, the sausages can be cooked after resting 30 minutes, but it's best to leave them at cool room temperature 2 hours for the casings to dry. They can then be put in a resealable bag, or tightly wrapped in plastic wrap, and refrigerated 2 days to let the flavors develop. The sausages will keep up to 1 week in the refrigerator.

1½ teaspoons fennel seeds
½ teaspoon kosher or sea salt
1 pound 2 ounces ground pork belly
2 teaspoons hot smoked paprika (*piménton*)
2 garlic cloves, crushed
1 tablespoon red wine vinegar
a little vegetable oil
freshly ground black pepper

YOU WILL ALSO NEED:
natural sausage casings

SERVES 4 | **PREPARATION TIME** 30 minutes, plus drying and chilling

FRESH CHORIZO SAUSAGES [*pictured overleaf*]

Chorizo is the spicy sausage famously used in Mexican and Spanish cooking. The key ingredient in chorizo is Spanish paprika, called *piménton*. The chilies used for *piménton* are smoked and dried, giving them a distinct flavor and a deep red color. You'll find *piménton* in most large supermarkets and delis, and it is also available online. This recipe makes a fresh chorizo sausage meat that needs cooking, unlike the air-dried alternative that can be eaten uncooked and is most commonly served as part of a tapas meal.

1] Grind the fennel seeds and salt together until as fine as possible, using a mini food processor or a mortar and pestle. Put the pork in a large bowl and add the fennel, salt, smoked paprika, garlic and vinegar. Mix together, then check the seasoning by frying 1 teaspoon in a little oil in a skillet. Add more salt, pepper or paprika, if you like.

2] To make the sausages, prepare the casings according to the producer's directions. If you have a manual sausage maker, follow the manufacturer's directions. Alternatively, fit a large pastry bag with a ½ to 1 inch plain tip. Tie a knot in one end of the sausage casing and insert the tip of the pastry bag into the other end, then feed the casing evenly over the tip. Fill the bag with the chorizo mixture, then squeeze firmly and evenly, forcing the chorizo filling into the sausage casing. You might find it easier to do this with two people, one holding and directing the casing and the other squeezing the bag. Tie the end of the casing, leaving a gap at the end.

3] Twist the casing at 4-inch intervals to form the sausage links. The sausages can be cooked after resting 30 minutes, but it's best to leave them at cool room temperature 2 hours to dry. They can then be put in a resealable bag, or tightly wrapped in plastic wrap, and refrigerated 2 days to let the flavors develop. The sausages will keep up to 1 week in the refrigerator.

1 pound 10 ounces boneless shoulder
  or Boston butt, cut into 1-inch cubes

½ teaspoon turmeric

½ teaspoon garam masala

¼ teaspoon cayenne pepper

¼ teaspoon salt

1 onion, roughly chopped

2 fresh green chilies, seeded and
  roughly chopped

4 garlic cloves, peeled

1-inch piece gingerroot, peeled and
  roughly chopped

1 tablespoon vegetable oil

1 tablespoon cumin seeds

¼ teaspoon mustard seeds

salt and freshly ground pepper

boiled basmati rice, to serve

SERVES 4 to 6 | **PREPARATION TIME** 15 minutes, plus marinating |
COOKING TIME 2 hours 10 minutes

COORG PORK CURRY

Coorg, or *pandi*, curry is a popular dish in the Kodagu region of southwest India. It is traditionally served with rice dumplings, but is also excellent with basmati rice.

1] Put the pork in a bowl and sprinkle the turmeric, garam masala, cayenne pepper and salt over. Toss the pork to coat it in the spices, then cover and leave to marinate 30 minutes.

2] Put the onion, chilies, garlic and ginger into a food processor or blender and blitz to a paste, then leave to one side.

3] Put the oil in a medium-sized Dutch oven or a heavy-bottomed saucepan over high heat. When the oil is shimmering, add the pork and fry 5 to 6 minutes, turning the pork regularly, until brown on the outside.

4] Add the onion paste and cook, stirring, 5 minutes. Pour in ½ cup water. Bring to a boil, then turn down the heat to very low, cover and simmer 1½ hours until the pork is tender enough to cut easily with a table knife. Remove the lid and simmer the curry 30 minutes longer, stirring occasionally, until the sauce thickens.

5] Meanwhile, toast the cumin and mustard seeds in a dry skillet 3 to 4 minutes until the cumin starts to release its aroma and turns slightly darker in color.

6] Grind the spices to a powder in a mini food processor or using a mortar and pestle, then stir them into the curry at the end of the cooking time. Season with salt and pepper, to taste, and serve with basmati rice.

1 teaspoon cumin seeds

1 teaspoon coriander seeds

1/2 teaspoon mustard seeds

1 teaspoon red pepper flakes

1/2 teaspoon black peppercorns

8 garlic cloves, crushed

2-inch piece gingerroot, peeled and grated

2 tablespoons red wine vinegar

2 1/4 pounds fresh boneless pork leg,
  cut into 1-inch cubes

2 tablespoons vegetable oil

2 onions, thinly sliced

2 fresh red chilies, seeded and chopped

1 1/4 cups vegetable stock

2 tablespoons tomato paste

salt

boiled basmati rice or naan breads and
  mango chutney (optional), to serve

SERVES 4 | **PREPARATION TIME** 20 minutes, plus overnight marinating | **COOKING TIME** 1 hour 20 minutes

PORK VINDALOO

Pork is the meat traditionally used in a Goan vindaloo curry. This is a particularly good version and is not overwhelmingly hot, but aromatic and slightly tangy. If you can get dried Kashmiri chilies use six of them, roughly chopped, instead of the pepper flakes.

1] Toast the cumin, coriander and mustard seeds with the red pepper flakes and peppercorns in a dry skillet 3 to 4 minutes until they smell aromatic. Grind the spices in a mini food processor or using a mortar and pestle. Transfer to a large bowl and mix in the garlic, ginger and vinegar. Add the pork and toss to coat it in the spice paste. Cover and leave to marinate in the refrigerator 8 hours, or overnight.

2] Put the oil in a large Dutch oven or a heavy-bottomed saucepan over medium heat. Add the onions and cook 8 to 10 minutes, stirring occasionally, until soft. Add the red pepper flakes and cook 1 minute, then add the pork and cook 6 to 8 minutes longer, turning the pieces of pork regularly, until the pork is brown on the outside.

3] Stir in the stock and tomato paste and bring to a boil, then turn down the heat to very low, cover and simmer 40 minutes, stirring occasionally. Uncover the casserole and cook 10 to 15 minutes longer until the sauce slightly thickens.

4] Season with salt to taste, then serve the curry with basmati rice. Mango chutney is also a good accompaniment, because its sweetness balances the slight sourness of the vinegar in the curry.

1 fresh mild green chili, seeded and chopped

2-inch piece gingerroot, peeled and grated

8 cardamom pods, seeds removed and pods discarded

½ teaspoon ground cumin

½ teaspoon ground coriander

scant 1 cup Greek-style yogurt, plus extra to serve

1 pound 10 ounces fresh boneless pork leg, cut into 1-inch cubes

7 tablespoons unsalted butter

2 onions, chopped

1 cinnamon stick, about 4 inches long

scant 1 cup heavy cream

1 handful cilantro leaves

salt and freshly ground black pepper

1 recipe quantity Buttered Rice (see page 217) or plain boiled basmati rice, to serve

SERVES 4 | **PREPARATION TIME** 20 minutes, plus overnight marinating | **COOKING TIME** 1 hour 25 minutes

PORK KORMA

The yogurt adds a very elegant finish to this popular mild curry.

1] Grind the chili, ginger and cardamom seeds in a blender and blitz to a paste using a mini food processor or mortar and pestle. Transfer the paste to a large bowl and stir in the cumin, ground coriander and yogurt. Add the pork and toss to coat it in the marinade. Cover and leave to marinate in the refrigerator 8 hours, or overnight.

2] Preheat the oven to 350°F. Melt the butter in a medium-sized Dutch oven or a heavy-bottomed saucepan over medium heat. Add the onions and cook 8 to 10 minutes, stirring, until soft. Add the pork and marinade and cook 5 to 7 minutes longer, turning occasionally, until the pork is brown on the outside.

3] Add ½ cup water and the cinnamon stick, then cover, transfer the pan to the oven and cook 40 minutes. Check after 20 minutes, giving the curry a stir and adding an extra splash of water if it looks dry.

4] Remove the pan from the oven and stir in the cream. Re-cover the pan and return it to the oven 20 minutes longer.

5] Season with salt and pepper to taste, then scatter the cilantro leaves over. Serve topped with a spoonful of yogurt and with buttered rice.

5 shallots, roughly chopped

2 garlic cloves, roughly chopped

1-inch piece gingerroot, peeled and roughly chopped

2 fresh red Thai or serrano chilies

1 tablespoon vegetable oil

2¼ pounds fresh boneless pork leg, cut into 1-inch cubes

1 cup canned coconut milk

2 lemongrass stalks, tough outer leaves removed, bruised

5 cardamom pods

3 kaffir lime leaves

1 cinnamon stick, about 4 inches long

1 star anise

1 tablespoon soy sauce

1 tablespoon soft dark brown sugar

4 tablespoons unsweetened shredded coconut, toasted (optional)

1 handful cilantro leaves

COCONUT RICE

1 cup jasmine or basmati rice

⅔ cup canned coconut milk

salt

SERVES 4 to 6 | PREPARATION TIME 30 minutes | COOKING TIME 1 hour 50 minutes

INDONESIAN CURRIED PORK WITH COCONUT RICE

This recipe is based on *Rendang*, which is an aromatic, chili-hot curry that originated in Indonesia, but is now popular all over Southeast Asia. It is not a typical curry since there is very little sauce, instead the meat is infused with the intense flavor of the spices. If you want a less spicy version, remove the seeds from the chilies before making the paste.

1] Put the shallots, garlic, ginger and chilies into a blender or food processor and blend to a paste.

2] Put the oil in a wok or large skillet with a lid over medium heat. When the oil is shimmering, add the paste and fry 2 minutes, stirring. Next, add the pork and cook 5 to 6 minutes, turning occasionally, until it is brown all over.

3] Add the coconut milk and aromatics to the wok and bring to a boil. Turn down the heat to low, cover and simmer 45 minutes. Uncover the wok, stir in the soy sauce and sugar, then simmer 45 to 55 minutes longer until there is no liquid left in the wok and the pork is sizzling.

4] Meanwhile, put the rice in a strainer and rinse under cold running water until it runs clear. Leave to drain 2 minutes, then transfer to a medium-sized saucepan and add the coconut milk and 1 cup water. Bring to a boil and add a pinch of salt, then turn down the heat to its lowest setting, cover and simmer gently 10 minutes until there is no liquid left in the pan and the rice is tender. Turn off the heat and leave the rice to stand, still covered, 10 minutes, then fluff up the rice with a fork.

5] Serve the pork with the coconut rice, scattered with toasted coconut, if using, and the cilantro.

2¾ pounds pork spareribs, cut individually

1 teaspoon paprika

½ cup rice wine vinegar

½ cup soy sauce

1½ cups vegetable stock

1 bay leaf

12 peppercorns

3 garlic cloves, peeled

1 tablespoon cornstarch

1 tablespoon honey

2 tablespoons vegetable oil

2 scallions, thinly sliced

freshly ground black pepper

boiled jasmine or basmati rice, to serve

SERVES 4 | **PREPARATION TIME** 20 minutes, plus marinating | **COOKING TIME** 1¾ hours

FILIPINO SWEET & SOUR PORK

Filipino cooking takes its influences from many parts of the world. Considered the national dish of the Philippines, this dish, otherwise known as *adobo*, takes its name from the Spanish word for "marinade," and is typically a balance of sweet, sour and salty flavors.

1] Put the ribs in a bowl and sprinkle with the paprika. Season with ground black pepper and pour the vinegar and soy sauce over. Turn to coat the ribs in the marinade and leave to marinate 30 minutes.

2] Put a large Dutch oven or a heavy-bottomed saucepan over medium heat. Add the ribs, marinade and vegetable stock; the liquid should come halfway up the ribs, so if there isn't enough add water. Add the bay leaf and peppercorns. Roughly crush the garlic cloves with the back of a knife and add to the casserole.

3] Bring the liquid to a boil, then turn down the heat to very low, cover and simmer 1 to 1½ hours until the pork is tender. Turn the ribs over every 30 minutes.

4] Remove the cooked ribs and pat dry with paper towels. Skim any fat from the surface of the sauce, then bring to a boil and boil until it reduces by half. Mix the cornstarch with 1 tablespoon water, then whisk this into the sauce with the honey. Return the sauce to a boil and boil 1 to 2 minutes until it thickens slightly. Keep the sauce warm.

5] Put the oil in large skillet over medium-high heat. Add the ribs and cook until brown all over. Transfer to a large serving bowl and pour the sauce over. Sprinkle with the scallion slices and serve with jasmine rice.

CHAPTER 4

SLOW-COOKED

Cooking slow and low is a technique that suits many dishes, from slow-roasting a pork belly in a low oven, or braising a ham hock in a little wine, to the gentle simmering of a hearty stew. Yet, they all yield the same result—moist, tender, flavorful meat. Like most meats, the best cuts of pork for slow cooking are the tougher ones: the muscles that do the most work. They usually have a high proportion of marbled fat and connective tissue and these melt into the cooking liquid, resulting in an unctuous sauce. Try Pork Cheeks with Caramelized Fennel to see how a cut that looks quite unpromising can become a restaurant-worthy dish, or Sticky Barbecue Ribs for pork so tender it literally falls off the bone.

Slow-cooked pork also has the advantage of needing very little attention during cooking, while still producing some impressively good dishes. Who can resist Slow-Roasted Pork Belly with its crisp cracklings or an Eight-Hour Roasted Shoulder of Pork so tender it can be cut with a fork? Any festive table will also welcome Homecooked Ham in Ginger & Mustard Glaze.

Slow-cooked dishes also reheat well and are often best if cooled, stored in the refrigerator and then reheated the next day. Try Pork Goulash for an excellent family meal or Chinese Pork Belly with Seasoned Rice for something slightly more stylish. Whatever dish you choose to make, you'll find slow cooking is a wonderful and satisfying way to prepare pork.

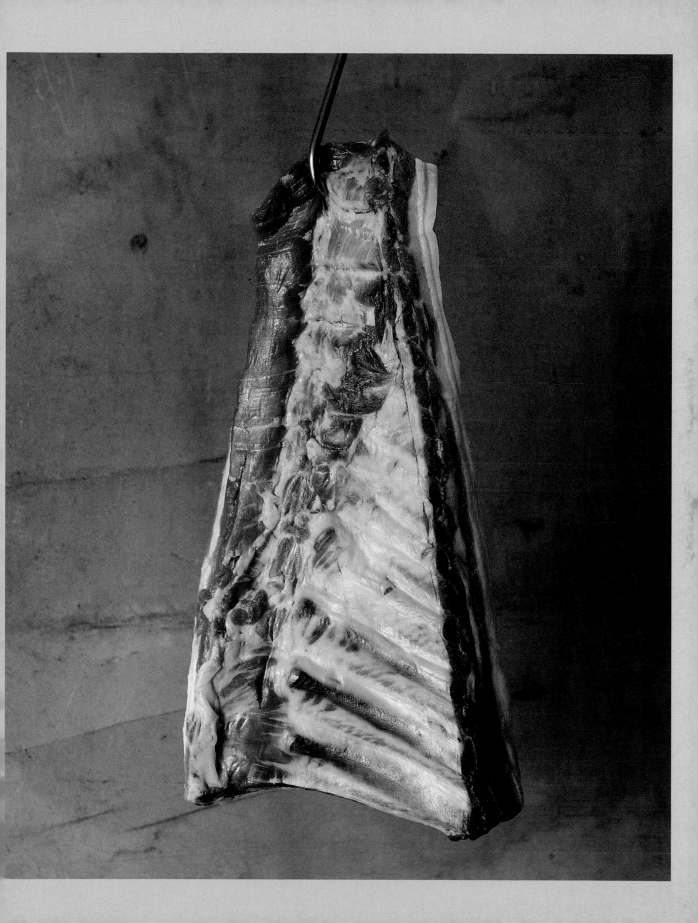

SLOW-COOKED

4 pig ears, trimmed
1 onion, quartered
1 carrot, scrubbed and halved
1 celery stalk, halved
6 black peppercorns
1 thyme sprig
1 bay leaf

½ cup all-purpose flour
vegetable oil, for deep-frying
cayenne pepper, to season
salt
1 recipe quantity Applesauce (see page 213),
   or a green salad dressed in lemon and olive
   oil, to serve

SERVES 4 | **PREPARATION TIME** 30 minutes, plus cooling | **COOKING TIME** 2 hours

CRISP PIG EARS

A very popular dish whenever it's on the menu. This often unused part of the pig has a fantastic texture when fried until crisp.

1] Wash the ears thoroughly and put them in a large saucepan. Cover with cold water and add the onion, carrot, celery, peppercorns, thyme and bay leaf. Bring to a boil over high heat, then skim any foamy scum that rises to the surface. Cover the pan, turn down the heat to low and simmer 1½ hours until the ears are very soft. Drain the ears, discarding the solids, and leave them to cool to room temperature.

2] Put the ears on a large cutting board and cut them into ⅛-inch-wide strips. Pat the strips as dry as possible with paper towels.

3] Pour enough oil in a deep saucepan or deep-fat fryer to fill by one-third. Heat the oil to 350°F. Line a baking sheet with a double layer of paper towels.

4] Put the flour into a bowl. Take a small handful of the ear strips and toss them in the flour, then carefully drop them, a couple at a time, into the hot oil. Take care because the ears are likely to spit as they go into the oil. Fry 2 minutes until crisp and golden brown. Using a slotted spoon, scoop the cooked strips out of the fat and transfer to the lined baking sheet to drain. Cook the remaining ear strips in batches, making sure the oil is reheated to the correct temperature between batches.

5] Season the cooked strips with cayenne pepper and salt and serve with applesauce. Alternatively, scatter the strips over a dressed green salad.

2 cups leftover shredded cooked pork from Eight-Hour Roasted Shoulder of Pork recipe (see page 170)

5 tablespoons plum sauce

16 rice paper wrappers, about 8½ inches in diameter

1 large handful mint leaves

1 large handful basil leaves

1 large handful cilantro leaves

1 cucumber, seeded and cut into matchsticks

2 large carrots, cut into matchsticks

1 bunch scallions, sliced into thin strips lengthwise

DIPPING SAUCE

4 tablespoons sugar

4 tablespoons lime juice

4 tablespoons fish sauce

2 fresh green Thai or serrano chilies, thinly sliced

SERVES 4 (makes 16) | **PREPARATION TIME** 40 minutes, plus Eight-Hour Roasted Shoulder of Pork and chilling

VIETNAMESE PORK SUMMER ROLLS

This simple dish uses the leftovers from the Eight-Hour Roasted Shoulder of Pork, but you can also use any slowly cooked pork tender enough to be shredded with a fork. The rolls are also good with sweet chili sauce if you don't want to make the dip.

1] Mix together the pork and plum sauce in a bowl. Set out a large bowl of warm water, a cutting board or tray lined with paper towels and a second cutting board for forming the rolls. It is easiest to make the rolls one at a time. Line a baking sheet with waxed paper and leave to one side

2] Soak a rice paper wrapper in warm water 1 to 2 minutes until soft. Transfer it to the board lined with paper towels and blot away any excess water, then carefully lift the wrapper onto the second board. Lay a couple of mint leaves in a row along the middle of the wrapper, leaving a 1-inch border of rice wrapper on each side. Repeat with a couple basil leaves and 2 or 3 cilantro leaves. Spoon a heaped tablespoon of the pork on top of the herbs, then add a few pieces of cucumber, carrot and spring onions.

3] Fold the short sides of the wrapper over the filling, then carefully fold the bottom of the wrapper over the filling and roll up tightly. Transfer the roll to the prepared lined baking sheet. Repeat with the remaining wrappers and filling. Once all the rolls are made, cover with very lightly dampened paper towels and put in the refrigerator up to 2 hours.

4] To make the dip, mix all the ingredients together with 4 tablespoons warm water until the sugar dissolves, then refrigerate until needed.

5] To serve, divide the dipping sauce into small bowls. Cut each roll in half on the diagonal and serve with the sauce.

2 tablespoons olive oil

1 onion, finely chopped

1 carrot, finely diced

1 celery stalk, finely diced

2 garlic cloves, crushed

1 pound 2 ounces boneless pork shoulder
or Boston butt, cut into 1-inch cubes

2/3 cup red wine

1 can (15-oz.) crushed tomatoes

2/3 cup beef stock

4 thyme sprigs

6 juniper berries

14 ounces dry pappardelle

salt and freshly ground black pepper

freshly shredded Parmesan cheese, to serve

SERVES 4 | PREPARATION TIME 15 minutes | COOKING TIME 3 hours 45 minutes

PORK IN RED WINE WITH PAPPARDELLE

This is my version of the popular Tuscan *pappardelle al cinghiale*, or pasta with wild boar. Pork shoulder is an excellent alternative to wild boar, and like most slow-cooked dishes, the sauce is even better if chilled overnight and reheated the next day.

1] Put 1 tablespoon of the oil in a medium-sized Dutch oven or a heavy-bottomed saucepan over low heat. Add the onion, carrot, celery and garlic and cook 8 to 10 minutes, stirring occasionally, until the vegetables are soft but not colored. Transfer the vegetables to a plate and leave to one side.

2] Turn up the heat to medium-high. Add half of the remaining oil and brown the pork 6 to 8 minutes in two batches. Add the rest of the oil before cooking the second batch.

3] Return the vegetables and pork to the pan and pour in the wine. Bring to a boil and cook 5 to 8 minutes until the wine reduces by half, stirring occasionally to remove any brown sediment on the bottom of the pan. Add the tomatoes, stock, thyme and juniper berries. Return to a boil, then turn down the heat to very low and simmer, covered, 1½ hours, stirring occasionally.

4] Uncover the pan and continue to simmer very gently 1½ hours longer until the pork is falling to pieces and the sauce thickens. Stir occasionally, making sure the sauce doesn't catch on the bottom of the pan. Remove the pan from the heat and stir the sauce with a fork to tear the meat into small shreds. Remove the thyme stems and juniper berries and season with salt and pepper to taste. Keep the sauce warm.

5] Cook the pappardelle in a pan of boiling salted water about 12 minutes until al dente. Drain, reserving a cupful of the cooking water. Toss the pasta with the sauce, adding a little of the pasta cooking water if the sauce needs it. Serve with shredded Parmesan.

1 tablespoon soft light brown sugar
1 teaspoon paprika
1 teaspoon chili powder
1 teaspoon salt
1 teaspoon freshly ground black pepper
1/2 teaspoon cayenne pepper
5 pounds spareribs, preferably as a rack but
  can be cut individually
2 tablespoons vegetable oil
corn on the cob, baked potatoes and butter,
  to serve

BARBECUE SAUCE
1 1/4 cups tomato ketchup
scant 1 cup cola
1 tablespoon white wine vinegar
1 tablespoon honey
2 teaspoons Dijon mustard
1 teaspoon Worcestershire sauce

SERVES 4 | **PREPARATION TIME** 30 minutes, plus overnight marinating | **COOKING TIME** 3 1/4 hours

STICKY BARBECUE RIBS

This makes a great alternative to a Sunday roast or other big family meal. Putting the ribs in the oven early on a Sunday morning fills the house with the aromas of a great meal to come. The sharp, yet sweet, barbecue sauce is a must.

1] Mix together the sugar, paprika, chili powder, salt, pepper and cayenne pepper. Rub the mixture over both sides of the ribs, then cover and refrigerate 8 hours, or overnight.

2] To make the barbecue sauce, put all the ingredients in a medium-sized saucepan and bring to a boil, stirring frequently. Turn down the heat slightly and simmer about 20 minutes until the sauce reduces by half. Leave the sauce to cool, then refrigerate until needed. (The sauce can be made up to 5 days in advance.)

3] Preheat the oven to 300°F. Put the oil in a large roasting pan over medium-high heat. When the oil is shimmering, roast the ribs 6 to 8 minutes until brown all over. Remove the pan from the heat and leave to cool slightly.

4] Divide the sauce into two equal portions, and set one half aside for serving. Remove the ribs from the pan, brush them with some of the remaining sauce, then return them to the pan, bones down. Cover the pan tightly with foil and roast 2 hours until the meat is very tender.

5] Increase the oven temperature to 425°F. Remove the foil and roast the ribs 40 minutes longer, brushing them with a little extra sauce and turning the pan every 10 minutes. (If the ribs are cut individually, roast them 30 minutes at this stage.)

6] Transfer the ribs to a platter, separating them if necessary. Serve with the boiled sauce, corn on the cob and baked potatoes topped with butter. Have plenty of napkins handy!

"SHOW ME HOW" TO MARINATE THE RIBS

4½ pounds boneless pork shoulder or Boston butt roast, skin scored, rolled and tied with string

1 to 2 teaspoons vegetable oil

1 teaspoon fennel seeds

1 teaspoon coarse sea salt

2 celery stalks

1 large carrot, quartered lengthwise

1 onion, quartered

1 lemon, thinly sliced

1 cup dry white wine

1 cup vegetable stock

2 teaspoons cornstarch

freshly ground black pepper

1 recipe quantity Johnnie's Mashed Potatoes (see page 215) or Goose Fat Roast Potatoes (see page 216) and green vegetables, to serve

SERVES 4 (with leftovers) | PREPARATION TIME 20 minutes | COOKING TIME 8 hours 35 minutes

EIGHT-HOUR ROASTED SHOULDER OF PORK

Slow-roasted pork is fantastically easy, because it pretty much looks after itself. The slow cooking results in meat so tender it can be cut with a fork. It makes sense to cook a large roast so there are leftovers to make the Vietnamese Pork Summer Rolls (see page 166), or mix with barbecue sauce (see page 168) and serve in a soft roll.

1] Preheat the oven to 425°F. Pat the skin of the pork dry with paper towels, then rub it all over with a little oil. Grind the fennel seeds and salt together using a mini food processor or mortar and pestle and add plenty of black pepper. Rub the mixture all over the pork, making sure it gets into the cuts in the skin.

2] Put the celery, carrot and onion in the bottom of a medium-sized roasting tin. Scatter the lemon slices over and sit the pork on top. Roast 30 minutes until the skin starts to blister and crackle. Reduce the oven temperature to 250°F and tip the wine into the roasting pan. Roast the pork 8 hours longer, turning the pan around halfway through the cooking time. The pork is ready when it is so tender that you can pull pieces away with a fork and the cracklings is crisp.

3] Transfer the pork to a warm plate to rest. Strain the juices in the roasting pan through a strainer into a saucepan, discarding the lemon slices. Press the vegetables through the strainer with the back of a wooden spoon to extract as much liquid as possible. Add the stock and put the pan over low heat. Mix the cornstarch with 2 teaspoons water, then whisk it into the pan. Bring to a boil, stirring, then turn the heat down and simmer 1 minute until it thickens. Strain the gravy into a warm gravy boat.

4] Remove the string from the pork and cut off the cracklings. Cut or tear the pork into chunks and break the cracklings into pieces. Serve the pork and cracklings with the gravy, mashed potatoes and green vegetables.

1 pound 10 ounces boneless pork shoulder
   or Boston butt, cut into 1-inch cubes
rice or tortillas, cilantro leaves and lime
   wedges, to serve

SPICE PASTE
1½ teaspoons coriander seeds
½ teaspoon black peppercorns
½ teaspoon cumin seeds
3 whole cloves
½ teaspoon salt
½ teaspoon turmeric

½ teaspoon ancho chili powder
   or chili powder
½ teaspoon dried oregano
5 garlic cloves, crushed
4 tablespoons fresh orange juice
4 tablespoons fresh lime juice

PINEAPPLE SALSA
¼ large ripe pineapple, skin removed,
   cored and finely diced
1 small red onion, minced
juice of 1 lime

SERVES 4 | PREPARATION TIME 20 minutes, plus overnight marinating | COOKING TIME 3 hours

MEXICAN PORK SHOULDER

The combination of aromatics gives a distinctive taste to this slow-roasted pork, while the kick from the pineapple salsa is guaranteed to set your taste buds tingling!

1] To make the spice paste, toast the coriander seeds, peppercorns, cumin seeds and cloves in a dry skillet over medium heat and toast until they smell aromatic. Grind using a mini food processor or mortar and pestle, then transfer to a nonmetallic bowl and mix in the remaining paste ingredients. Add the pork and turn it in the paste until evenly coated. Cover the bowl tightly and marinate overnight in the refrigerator.

2] Preheat the oven to 325°F. Line a large roasting pan with foil, leaving a good overhang, then line the foil with a similar size sheet of parchment paper. Spread the pork out in the lined pan, fold the parchment paper and foil over the pork, then scrunch the edges of the foil together to form a sealed package. Bake 3 hours until the pork is very tender and it can be cut with a fork.

3] While the pork is cooking, mix together all the ingredients for the pineapple salsa in a nonmetallic bowl and leave to one side.

4] Put the pork on a serving platter and flake it into pieces with a fork. You can spoon it onto cooked rice or serve with tortillas, adding spoonfuls of salsa, a few cilantro leaves and a squeeze of lime juice.

2¼ pounds boneless pork loin roast, skin and fat removed, and silverskin trimmed

4 tablespoons fennel seeds

6¼ cups coarse kosher or sea salt

2 egg whites

1 fennel bulb, trimmed and sliced

boiled fingerling potatoes, to serve

FENNEL & ORANGE SALAD

2 large fennel bulbs, trimmed and sliced crosswise

2 oranges, peeled and segmented

finely grated zest of 1 orange

2 tablespoons extra virgin olive oil

salt and freshly ground black pepper

SERVES 4 | **PREPARATION TIME** 20 minutes, plus resting | **COOKING TIME** 1½ hours

PORK LOIN IN A SALT & FENNEL CRUST

Baking in a salt crust is a traditional Mediterranean method of cooking. It is an excellent way of retaining moisture in pork, leaving it juicy, tender and perfectly seasoned. Here I suggest serving the pork with a fragrant fennel and orange salad, although spinach sautéed in a little butter is also delicious.

1] Preheat the oven to 250°F. Make sure all the fat, connective tissue and silverskin has been removed from the pork, then season all over with pepper.

2] To make the salt and fennel crust, roughly grind the fennel seeds using a mini food processor or mortar and pestle. Put the coarse salt in a large bowl. Whisk the egg whites until slightly frothy, then stir them into the salt with the ground fennel seeds until combined.

3] Put a ½-inch-thick layer of the salt mixture in the bottom of a roasting pan. Lay the fennel slices on top, making a bed of fennel just slightly larger than the pork. Sit the pork on top, then pack the remaining salt over and around the pork, forming a thick crust. Roast 1½ hours. If you want to check the pork after this time, insert a thin metal skewer through the crust and into the middle of the meat—the pork is cooked when the juices run clear.

4] Meanwhile, to make the salad, arrange the fennel and orange slices on a large platter, season with a little salt and pepper and drizzle with the olive oil. Leave to one side until ready to serve.

5] Remove the pan from the oven and leave the pork to rest 30 minutes. Use a knife to break through the crust, then transfer the pork to a board and brush away any residual salt. Cut the pork into thin slices. Serve with fingerling potatoes and the fennel and orange salad.

"SHOW ME HOW" TO MAKE THE SALT CRUST

6 fresh beets

2¼ pounds boneless pork loin roast

3 garlic cloves, sliced

2 tablespoons vegetable oil

4 or 5 large handfuls unsprayed hay

½ cup crème fraîche or sour cream

2 tablespoons freshly grated horseradish

a squeeze of lemon juice

salt and freshly ground black pepper

boiled fingerling potatoes, to serve

SERVES 4 | **PREPARATION TIME** 20 minutes | **COOKING TIME** 2 hours

HAY-ROASTED PORK LOIN

Roasting in hay is a very old cooking technique. The hay provides moisture and also acts as insulation, letting the meat cook gently in the residual heat of the oven. You can buy unsprayed hay, which is pesticide free, from a pet store.

1] Put the beets in a saucepan and cover with cold water. Bring up to a boil, then turn down the heat slightly and blanch 25 minutes; drain. The beets will not be completely tender at this point.

2] Meanwhile, preheat the oven to 250°F. Using a sharp knife, remove the skin and most of the fat from the pork. If you want the pork to keep a nice round shape, tie it with 3 or 4 pieces of string. Using a sharp knife, make slits in the pork and insert a slice of garlic into each one, pushing it into the meat. Season the pork with salt and pepper. Put the oil in a large skillet over high heat. When the oil is shimmering, add the pork and brown it all over, including the ends.

3] Put a handful of hay in the bottom of a large Dutch oven or a heavy-bottomed saucepan with an ovenproof handle and lid. Sit the pork on the hay and surround it with the partly cooked beets. Pack more hay around and over the top of the pork and beets. Cover the casserole.

4] Put the casserole in the oven and cook 45 minutes, then turn off the oven, leaving the door slightly ajar, and let the pork and beets sit in the oven 45 minutes longer. Remove the beets and peel away the skins and slice thinly.

5] Mix together the crème fraîche and horseradish, then season with some salt and a squeeze of lemon juice.

6] Remove the pork from the hay. Slice it thinly and serve with the beets and a spoonful of the horseradish crème fraîche. Fingerling potatoes alongside are perfect.

"SHOW ME HOW" TO STUD THE LOIN AND ROAST IN HAY

2¾ pounds boneless pork loin roast, skin
  and fat removed
4 pounds boneless pork belly
3 rosemary sprigs
leaves from 8 thyme sprigs
10 garlic cloves, peeled
finely grated zest of 1 lemon
1½ teaspoons coarse kosher or sea salt,
  plus extra for sprinkling

12 sage leaves
1 to 2 teaspoons vegetable oil
freshly ground black pepper
1 recipe quantity Goose Fat Roast Potatoes
  (see page 216), Applesauce (see page 213)
  and green vegetables, to serve

SERVES 8 to 10 | **PREPARATION TIME** 40 minutes, plus 2 hours standing and resting |
COOKING TIME 2¼ hours

PORCHETTA WITH HERBS & GARLIC

Porchetta was originally a boned, stuffed and rolled whole hog, most commonly cooked
for feasts and festivals. Using pork loin wrapped in a piece of pork belly captures the
best parts of this traditional dish; the fattier belly yields plenty of crisp skin and protects
the leaner loin, keeping it deliciously moist. You will need to buy pieces of meat that are
relatively the same size and it is a good idea to ask a butcher to help with this, but
it is well worth the effort for this truly celebratory roast. And applesauce is a must!

1] Using a sharp knife, trim away any excess meat from the side of the loin to leave a nice
round piece of meat, often referred to as the "eye". (The trimmed part of the pork loin
can be sliced thinly and used in a stir-fry.) Score the skin of the belly at ¼-inch intervals
(or ask a butcher to do this for you), taking care not to cut into the flesh. Turn the belly
over and make long cuts down the length of the flesh, then make several long cuts
along the width.

2] Finely chop the needles from two of the rosemary sprigs, then grind with the thyme,
garlic, lemon zest and salt using a mini food processor or mortar and pestle to make
a coarse paste. Season with plenty of pepper. Rub the herb paste into the flesh side
of the pork belly, making sure it gets into the cuts and the meat is evenly coated, then
arrange the sage leaves on top of the paste-coated flesh.

3] Sit the loin on top of the herb-rubbed belly and bring the edges of the belly together
to wrap around the loin. Tie the roast at 2-inch intervals with string, then sit it on a wire
rack over a roasting pan. Pat the skin dry with paper towels and leave to stand at room
temperature 2 hours.

4] Preheat the oven to 425°F.

5] Just before roasting, rub the skin of the porchetta with a little vegetable oil, then using a sharp paring knife, make small holes in the skin. Insert the needles from the remaining rosemary sprig into the holes and season with extra salt and a little pepper.

6] Put the porchetta back on the wire rack set over the roasting pan. Roast 45 minutes, turning the pan halfway through the time, until the skin begins to blister and crackle. Reduce the oven temperature to 300°F and roast 1½ hours longer. (If your porchetta is significantly bigger, then allow 40 minutes per 2¼ pounds or 18 minutes per pound of the total weight.) Remove the porchetta from the oven and check the pork is cooked through by inserting a metal skewer into the middle—the juices should run clear. If the juices are red, return to the oven 5 minutes, then test again. Leave to rest 30 minutes.

7] Traditionally, porchetta is cut into ½-inch-thick slices (with cracklings attached), but if you like thinner slices, remove the cracklings before carving the meat.

8] Serve the porchetta with goose fat roast potatoes, applesauce and green vegetables. Leftover cold porchetta makes the most fantastic filling for a sandwich.

JOHNNIE'S TIP

The porchetta can be assembled the day before serving and stored in the refrigerator. Make sure you remove it from the refrigerator, however, 2 hours before roasting. Leave it to stand, uncovered, at room temperature. Pat dry the skin thoroughly with paper towels after 1 hour to remove any condensation that can collect on the skin.

SLOW-COOKED

1¾ pounds boneless pork loin roast, skin and most of the fat removed

1 tablespoon unsalted butter

1 teaspoon vegetable oil

2 cups whole milk

3 long strips lemon peel pared from ½ lemon

1 garlic clove, peeled but left whole

1 bay leaf

1 thyme sprig

salt and freshly ground black pepper

1 recipe quantity Goose Fat Roast Potatoes (see page 216) and Green Beans with Garlic & Almonds (see page 218), to serve

SERVES 4 to 6 | PREPARATION TIME 15 minutes, plus resting | COOKING TIME 1¾ hours

SLOW-COOKED PORK IN MILK

Cooking the pork in milk keeps it moist and helps to tenderize the meat. The milk also cooks down into a thick sauce that is intensely flavored with lemon, garlic and thyme. I have used a boneless pork loin for ease, but you can also use a bone-in loin if you have a large enough Dutch oven.

1] Season the pork all over with salt and pepper. If you want the pork to keep a nice round shape, tie it with 3 or 4 pieces of string.

2] Put the butter and oil into a Dutch oven or a heavy-bottomed saucepan that is large enough to hold the pork snugly and place over medium heat. When foaming, add the pork and brown all over, not forgetting the ends.

3] Pour the milk into the pan; it should come halfway up the sides of the pork, so you might need slightly more or slightly less depending on the size of your casserole. Add the strips of lemon peel, the garlic, bay leaf and thyme. Bring to a boil, then turn down the heat to very low, partially cover and simmer 1 hour, turning the pork over every 20 minutes. The milk might curdle, but this is normal.

4] Uncover the pan and cook the pork 30 minutes longer until the sauce reduces right down and turns a light caramel color. Stir the sauce very regularly during this stage, because it can burn very quickly. Check the seasoning, adding extra salt and pepper to taste.

5] Remove the pork from the sauce and leave to rest, covered, 20 minutes, then remove the string, if used, cut into thin slices and set out on a platter. Gently reheat the sauce and spoon it over the pork. Serve with goose fat roast potatoes and green beans with garlic and almonds. The pork is also exceptionally good served cold.

HOW TO CONFIT PORK

Before the days of the refrigerator, storing cooked meat in fat, or confiting, was a way to preserve it. Meat preserved this way was also found to be flavorful, succulent and tender, so confiting has continued to be popular long after it ceased being a necessity.

Because confit meat can be reheated quickly and used in small quantities, it's a great way of adding an extra boost of flavor to lots of different dishes, such as a cassoulet, or used as a filling for ravioli (see page 184), or fried briefly and added to salads, stir-fries, paellas or risottos.

Because the meat takes a long bath in the fat, the best cuts to use are the ones suited to slow cooking, so pork belly and shoulder or Boston butt are ideal. The gentle cooking in fat breaks down the long fibers in the muscles, turning them from tough to tender and preventing the meat from drying out. For the confit, you can use lard, or rendered pork fat, but both goose and duck fat are also suitable, give great flavor and are sold in supermarkets.

Key to all methods of meat preservation, however, is to remove moisture, as food-spoiling bacteria need water to grow in. So, the first step in making a confit is to salt the meat to draw out any liquid. It also helps to prevent the meat from becoming too soft and completely collapsing during cooking. Because the salt needs to penetrate the meat, the length of time for salting depends on how thick the cut is, so it is often easier in a domestic kitchen to confit a couple of smaller pieces of pork rather than one large roast.

Once the salt is rinsed off, the pork is ready to cook. There needs to be enough fat to cover the meat completely, so a deep baking dish is required, and, again, smaller pieces are the most practical for confiting. Flavorings can be added to the fat, but they need to be quite robust to stand up to the fat and heat, so peppercorns, garlic, thyme, strips of lemon peel, mace, star anise and bay are the most popular. The pork is submerged in fat (which is warmed until melted on the stovetop), then covered with a piece of parchment paper to make sure it stays submerged and transferred to a low oven for however long specified in the recipe.

Once the pork is cooked, it can be left to cool slightly, then transferred to a clean, resealable container. For the best keeping qualities, any meat juices that have collected below the fat should be removed, but this is not essential if the confit pork is going to be refrigerated and used within a couple of weeks. The cooked meat should be completely submerged in the cooking fat, then covered and put in the refrigerator. For the best flavor, keep the confit at least one week in the refrigerator before using. It can be refrigerated up to one month as long as the meat is completely submerged in the fat.

1 pound 2 ounces boneless pork belly

4 tablespoons coarse kosher or sea salt

10 black peppercorns

1 star anise

6 garlic cloves, crushed but unpeeled

4 thyme sprigs

1 bay leaf

4 long strips lemon peel pared
  from ½ lemon

about 2¼ pounds goose fat

SERVES 2 or 4 as an appetizer | **PREPARATION TIME** 20 minutes, plus overnight chilling and leaving 1 week | **COOKING TIME** 3½ hours

CONFIT OF PORK BELLY [*pictured overleaf*]

1] Put the pork belly on a cutting board and rub the salt into the skin and flesh. Put the peppercorns, star anise, garlic, herbs and lemon peel in a nonmetallic container. Cover the meat and refrigerate overnight.

2] The next day, rinse the pork belly to remove the salt and aromatics and pat it dry thoroughly with a clean dish towel. Rinse the peppercorns, star anise, garlic, herbs and lemon rind to remove the salt and leave to one side.

3] Preheat the oven to 250°F. Put the reserved peppercorns, star anise, garlic, herbs and lemon rind in a Dutch oven or other ovenproof casserole and put the pork on top. Add the goose fat and warm on the stovetop until the fat becomes liquid. The pork should be submerged in the fat.

4] Cut a piece of parchment paper big enough to fit over the surface and press this on top. Put the casserole in the oven and cook for 2½–3 hours until the pork is very tender. Remove the casserole from the oven and leave the pork and fat to cool to room temperature, then transfer the pork to a resealable container. Strain over as much of the fat as you need to fully cover the pork. Discard the aromatics but any leftover fat can be kept and used again for another confit, or to roast potatoes in (see page 216). Cover the container and chill the pork at least 1 week before eating.

5] You can roast the pork briefly before serving, if you like, to crisp the skin. Preheat the oven to 350°F. Remove the pork from its container and scrape away as much fat as possible. Cut the pork into four portions and place on a baking sheet lined with paper towels. Roast 15 minutes, then turn up the oven temperature to 400°F and roast 5 minutes longer to crisp the skin.

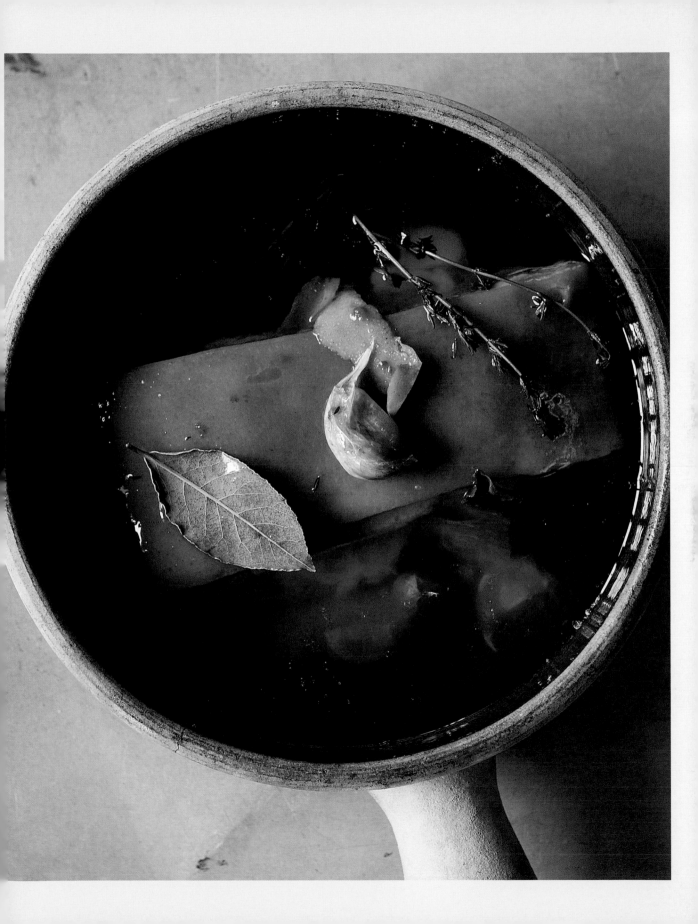

12/3 cups Italian OO flour, plus extra
   for dusting

3 eggs

1/2 recipe quantity Confit of Pork Belly
   (see page 181)

10 cornichons, finely chopped

2 large handfuls flat-leaf parsley leaves,
   chopped

finely grated zest of 1 lemon

salt and freshly ground black pepper

pea shoots or chopped parsley leaves,
   to serve

MADEIRA SAUCE

4 tablespoons cold unsalted butter, cubed

1 shallot, minced

4 tablespoons Madeira

1 cup beef stock

1/2 to 1 teaspoon lemon juice, to taste

SERVES 4 | PREPARATION TIME 1¾ hours, plus making Confit of Pork Belly, resting and chilling | COOKING TIME 35 minutes

RAVIOLI OF CONFIT PORK

A spectacular dish to be served only to your nearest and dearest! You need a pasta-making machine to roll out the dough.

1] To make the pasta dough, put the flour in a pile on a large work surface. Make a well in the middle and add one whole egg to the flour, then separate the remaining 2 eggs and add the yolks only. Using your fingertips, gradually incorporate the flour into the eggs to make a dough. If the dough is very dry or too stiff, then add a little of the leftover egg white, 1 teaspoon at a time, until it is slightly pliable. Knead about 5 minutes until the dough is smooth and silky. You can also make the dough in a food processor, adding all of the ingredients and processing until you get a smooth ball of dough. Wrap the dough in plastic wrap and leave it to rest at room temperature 30 minutes.

2] Meanwhile, remove the skin from the confit of pork belly and scrape away most of the fat. Shred and finely chop the meat with a little of the fat, then put it into a bowl. Mix in the cornichons, parsley and lemon zest. Season with a little salt and plenty of pepper.

3] Unwrap the pasta dough and divide into four equal pieces. Take one piece and re-wrap the remaining pieces until needed. Lightly dust a work surface with flour and set up the pasta-rolling machine. Line a large baking sheet with plastic wrap and generously dust it with flour. Feed the piece of dough through the widest setting of the pasta machine and repeat two or three times. Reduce the width between rollers by one notch, then feed the pasta through the rollers. Repeat, working down through the width settings until you have a long sheet of pasta. (If it becomes too long to work with, cut the pasta in half widthwise when you get to notch 5 on the machine, then roll the pieces separately.)

4] Using a 4¼-inch round cutter, cut out 6 circles of pasta. Lay out 3 circles and brush the edges with water. Put a heaped teaspoonful of the filling into the middle and lay a second pasta circle on top. Carefully press the top of the pasta around the filling to expel the air and seal the dough. Pinch the edges together with your fingers, then use the cutter to neaten, if you like. Transfer the ravioli to the prepared baking sheet and cover with plastic wrap. Repeat with the remaining pasta and filling, using a quarter of the pasta each time to prevent any drying out. The ravioli can be chilled up to 3 hours before cooking.

5] To make the sauce, melt 2 teaspoons of the butter in a saucepan over medium heat. When foaming, add the shallot and cook 6 to 8 minutes until soft. Add the Madeira, turn up the heat and boil until it reduces by half, then add the stock and boil 6 to 8 minutes until it reduces by about half again. Turn down the heat to very low, then gradually whisk in the remaining butter until you have a smooth, glossy sauce. Season with salt and pepper and stir in the lemon juice, to taste. Put the sauce in a warm place and whisk it regularly while you cook the pasta.

6] Bring a large saucepan of salted water to a boil. Carefully drop the ravioli into the water and return to a boil, then turn down the heat and simmer 5 minutes, turning them over halfway. Don't let the water boil rapidly, because it can break up the ravioli. You will need to cook them in two or three batches, depending on the size of your pan.

7] Gently reheat the sauce. Using a perforated spoon, lift the ravioli from the water and pat the bottom of the spoon dry with paper towels as you lift each one out. Serve the ravioli with the sauce spooned over and sprinkled with the pea shoots or parsley.

2¼ pounds boneless pork belly, skin scored

2-inch piece gingerroot, cut into ¼-inch-thick
  slices

4 scallions, trimmed

2 star anise

6 black peppercorns

3 tablespoons Chinese cooking wine
  or dry sherry

1 tablespoon soy sauce, plus extra to taste

1 teaspoon honey

1 recipe quantity Ginger Bok Choy
  (see page 217), to serve

SEASONED RICE

1 cup jasmine or basmati rice

3 tablespoons rice wine vinegar

2 tablespoons mirin

2 tablespoons sugar

a large pinch salt

SERVES 4 | **PREPARATION TIME** 20 minutes, plus cooling and overnight chilling |
COOKING TIME 7 hours over 2 days

CHINESE PORK BELLY WITH SEASONED RICE

This is a great dish for a dinner party because the pork can be braised a day or two ahead and finished just before serving. The pork belly can also be cut into smaller pieces to serve as a first course.

1] Preheat the oven to 300°F.

2] Put the pork belly in a large Dutch oven or a heavy-bottomed saucepan and add the ginger, scallions, star anise, peppercorns, cooking wine and soy sauce. Add enough water to just cover the pork (about 8 cups). If you don't have a large enough casserole, use a roasting pan and cover it with a double layer of foil before putting it in the oven.

3] Put the casserole over high heat and bring the liquid to a boil, then cover tightly with the lid and transfer to the oven. Cook 6 hours until the pork is very tender. Check the pork after 4 hours to see if the liquid needs topping up and add extra water, if needed. (Some will have evaporated, but it should still come halfway up the sides of the pork.)

4] Remove the casserole from the oven, uncover and leave the pork to cool 30 minutes. Use a pancake turner or large metal spatula to transfer the pork to a plate or baking sheet, but be careful because it is very tender and can break up. Leave to cool 30 minutes longer, then cover with a large plate or another baking sheet, weight the top with a couple filled cans and transfer to the refrigerator to chill overnight. Strain the cooking liquid into a container, leave to cool completely and then chill overnight, too.

5] To finish the dish the next day, preheat the oven to 350°F. Line a baking sheet with a piece of parchment paper. *[continued on page 188]*

6] Put the pork belly on a cutting board and, using a sharp knife, cut into four equal pieces. Put the pork, skin-side down, in a large, nonstick skillet. Put the pan over low heat 8 minutes until the fat starts to melt out of the pork. Increase the heat to medium-high and cook 4 to 5 minutes longer until the skin darkens slightly and turns crisp (take care, because it might spit a little at this point).

7] Transfer the pork to the prepared baking sheet, skin-side up, and put in the oven (reserving the fat from the pork in the skillet for future use). Cook 20 minutes, until the pork is heated through. Once the pork is hot, you can switch off the oven and leave the door slightly ajar and the pork will be fine sitting in the warm oven 20 minutes longer if you are not ready to serve it straightaway.

8] In the meanwhile, make the seasoned rice. Put the rice in a saucepan, then cover with water and season with salt. Put the pan over medium-high heat and bring to a boil. Turn the heat down to low, cover and simmer 8 to 10 minutes until the rice is tender. Drain the rice and return it to the saucepan. Stir in the vinegar, mirin, sugar and salt, then leave the pan to one side for a couple of minutes.

8] Skim and discard the fat that has settled on top of the pork cooking liquid, which should by now have gelled. Transfer the gelled mixture to a saucepan and bring to a boil over high heat. Boil 6 to 10 minutes until the liquid reduces by half to about ²/₃ cup. Keep the sauce warm.

9] Serve the pork on top of the rice and the ginger bok choy with the sauce spooned over.

JOHNNIE'S TIP

To finish the pork in Step 6, for a really restaurant-style appearance when cutting the meat into portions, make sure the belly is completely chilled. Using a large heavy, sharp knife, trim the sides of the belly to give it a neat finish, then cut into four equal portions ready for reheating. Any trimmings can be cut into dice and quickly stir-fried for adding to an oriental salad.

1 tablespoon vegetable oil

3 pounds 5 ounces to 4½ pounds bone-in pork belly, skin unscored

3 tablespoons coarse kosher or sea salt

2 onions, quartered

2 celery stalks, halved

2 carrots, halved lengthwise

1 recipe quantity Sticky Red Cabbage (see page 219), Apple Jam (see page 213) and Johnnie's Mashed Potatoes (see page 215), to serve

SERVES 4 | **PREPARATION TIME** 30 minutes, plus resting | **COOKING TIME** 12 hours

SLOW-ROASTED PORK BELLY [*pictured overleaf*]

This cracking dish was the catalyst for writing this book, and I have to say it's the most popular meal I have ever had the pleasure to serve. Meat always tastes best if it is roasted on the bone, and although unusually the skin isn't scored in this recipe, I find it gives the best results.

1] Preheat the oven to 425°F.

2] Massage the oil all over the pork and sprinkle the salt over the skin. It may look like a lot of salt, but it helps to draw the moisture out of the skin, giving fantastic crisp cracklings. Sit the pork, skin-side up, on a bed of onions, celery and carrots in a roasting tin.

3] Roast the pork belly 45 minutes until the skin starts to bubble and crackle at the edges. Turn the roasting pan, then reduce the oven temperature to 400°F. Roast 45 minutes longer, by which time there should be a bubbly glaze appearing on the skin. Now reduce the oven temperature to 350°F, turn the pan again and roast 45 minutes longer. Reduce the temperature to 300°F and roast 45 minutes, then reduce the temperature to 250°F and roast 45 minutes. Turn the roasting pan every time you reduce the oven temperature so the pork cooks evenly.

4] Finally, reduce the temperature to 200°F and roast 8 hours, turning the pan once again halfway through the cooking time. Remove the pan from the oven, scrape off the excess salt, then transfer the pork to a warm plate and leave to rest 20 minutes. Twist and pull out the bones and use a sharp knife to ease away the white cartilage attached to the meat. Serve the pork with sticky red cabbage, apple jam and mashed potatoes.

JOHNNIE'S TIP

If using a boneless pork belly, you will need a 2¼-pound piece. Sit the pork belly on a roasting rack or on a bed of carrots, onions and celery. Decrease the final cooking time at 200°F to 3 hours.

1 pound 2 ounces boneless pork belly, cut into
  2-inch cubes

4 large scallions, halved lengthwise

3-inch piece gingerroot, cut into
  $^1/_{16}$-inch-thick slices (no need to peel)

4 tablespoons mirin

4 tablespoons sake or dry sherry

4 tablespoons soy sauce

4 tablespoons soft light brown sugar

4 eggs

hot Japanese mustard (*karashi*) or English
  mustard, boiled white rice, steamed bok choy
  and shredded daikon (mooli) (optional),
  to serve

SERVES 4 | **PREPARATION TIME** 15 minutes | **COOKING TIME** 3$^1/_4$ hours

JAPANESE PORK BELLY

Pork belly is usually roasted to render some of the fat, but in this Japanese dish
it is braised very slowly to reduce the fattiness and leave lusciously moist meat. This
is perfect cold-weather food.

1] Put the pork belly in a medium-sized saucepan and cover with water. Add the scallions
and ginger and bring to a boil over high heat, skimming away any foam that rises to
the surface. Turn down the heat to low, cover the pan and simmer very gently
1$^1/_2$ hours until the meat is tender—it should start to fall apart when you prod it with
a fork. Remove the pork from the pan, reserving the cooking liquid, and pat dry with
paper towels.

2] Heat a wok or large skillet over medium heat. Add the pork and cook until brown (it will
spit and pop a little). Add the mirin, sake, soy sauce, sugar and $^1/_2$ cup of the reserved
cooking liquid and bring to a boil. Turn down the heat to low and press
a piece of parchment paper onto the surface of the liquid. Simmer 30 minutes, then
turn the pork over, re-cover the liquid with a piece of parchment paper and simmer
30 minutes longer. The pork should be very tender by this point. The Japanese say you
should be able to slide a chopstick easily through the fatty part of the pork.

3] Remove the paper from the wok. Turn up the heat very slightly and simmer the pork
25 to 30 minutes, turning regularly, until the sauce thickens to a coating consistency.
If the sauce becomes too sticky and syrupy, add a little of the reserved cooking liquid.

4] Meanwhile, hard-boil the eggs, then cool them slightly under cold running water and
shell. The Japanese tend to serve 3 or 4 pieces of pork per person in a small bowl with
a little of the sauce and topped with a halved hard-boiled egg and a spoonful of hot
mustard. Serve with white rice, bok choy and daikon, if you like.

1 tablespoon vegetable oil

3 pounds 5 ounces fresh boneless pork leg
   roast, fat scored

1 onion, thinly sliced

2 rosemary sprigs

2 thyme sprigs

1 cup red wine

6 garlic bulbs, left whole

1 to 2 teaspoons olive oil

salt and freshly ground black pepper

1 recipe quantity Johnnie's Mashed Potatoes
   (see page 215) and Sticky Red Cabbage
   (see page 219), to serve

SERVES 4 to 6 (with leftovers) | **PREPARATION TIME** 15 minutes | **COOKING TIME** 2½ hours

POT-ROASTED LEG OF PORK WITH SWEET GARLIC

Pork leg is not as fatty as the shoulder, so it can become dry when cooked. Pot-roasting keeps it moist, as well as providing plenty of delicious gravy.

1] Preheat the oven to 325°F. Put the oil in a large Dutch oven or a heavy-bottomed saucepan with an ovenproof handle and lid over medium heat. When the oil is shimmering, season the pork with salt and pepper and brown it on all sides, then transfer the pork to a plate.

2] Add the onion to the casserole and cook 4 to 5 minutes until it starts to become soft. Sit the pork on top of the onion, add the herbs and wine and bring to a boil. Cover the casserole, transfer it to the oven and cook 2 hours until the meat is tender.

3] Meanwhile, slice the top off each garlic bulb and peel away the papery outer skin. Sit each bulb on a square of foil and drizzle a little olive oil over the top. Bring the edges of the foil together and scrunch to seal the top, so each bulb is contained in a small package. Put the packages on a baking sheet and roast, on the shelf below the pork, 1 to 1¼ hours until the garlic is very soft.

4] Remove the pork and garlic from the oven. Transfer the pork to a plate. Increase the oven temperature to 425°F. Cut the skin away from the pork, put it on a baking sheet and roast 15 to 20 minutes until crisp. Meanwhile, cover the pork with foil to keep it warm and leave to rest.

5] Put the casserole over high heat and add 1 cup water. Bring to a boil, then turn down the heat down and simmer 1 minute, stirring. Check the seasoning, then strain the juices into a warm gravy boat, discarding the onion and herbs.

6] Carve the pork into thin slices and cut the cracklings into pieces. Serve the pork and cracklings with the gravy and the bulbs of garlic for squeezing over the meat. Mashed potatoes and sticky red cabbage are by far the best accompaniments.

4 tablespoons all-purpose flour

1 pound 10 ounces fresh boneless pork leg, cut into 1-inch cubes

1 tablespoon unsalted butter

1 large onion, thinly sliced

1 garlic clove, crushed

1 to 2 tablespoons vegetable oil

1 tablespoon paprika

1/2 teaspoon cayenne pepper

1/2 cup dry white wine

1 can (15-oz.) crushed tomatoes

1 cup vegetable stock

1 bay leaf

1 red bell pepper, seeded and cut in half lengthwise

4 tablespoons sour cream

1 handful flat-leaf parsley leaves, chopped

salt and freshly ground black pepper

basmati rice or 1 recipe quantity Buttered Rice (see page 217), to serve

SERVES 4 | **PREPARATION TIME** 15 minutes | **COOKING TIME** 2½ hours

PORK GOULASH

This is a great variation on the usual beef goulash recipe. For me, the pork adds more flavor to the sweet, slightly tangy creamy sauce.

1] Season the flour with plenty of salt and pepper in a large bowl. Toss the pork in the seasoned flour and transfer it to a plate, discarding any excess flour in the bowl.

2] Melt the butter in a large Dutch oven or a heavy-bottomed saucepan over medium heat. When foaming, add the onion and garlic and cook 8 to 10 minutes until soft. Transfer the onion to a plate and turn up the heat to medium-high.

3] Add 1 tablespoon of the oil to the casserole. When the oil is shimmering, add half the pork and brown on all sides. Using a slotted spoon, remove the pork to a plate and leave to one side, then brown the remaining pork.

4] Return the first batch of pork and the onion mixture to the pan with the paprika and cayenne. Cook 2 minutes, stirring, then add the wine and bring to a boil. Boil until the wine reduces by half, then add the tomatoes, stock and bay leaf. Return to a boil, then turn down the heat to low, partially cover the casserole and simmer about 2 hours until the pork is tender enough to cut with a fork.

5] Meanwhile, preheat the broiler to high. Broil the red pepper, skin-side up, 3 to 4 minutes until charred in places. Put the pepper in a bowl, cover tightly with plastic wrap and leave to cool. Peel away the skin, then cut the pepper into thin strips. Add the pepper strips to the goulash 30 minutes before the end of the cooking time.

6] Season the goulash with salt and pepper to taste. Remove the casserole from the heat, then serve the goulash topped with sour cream and parsley, and with rice by the side.

1 pound 2 ounces jarred or canned
  sauerkraut, drained

2 tablespoons unsalted butter

1 onion, thinly sliced

2 garlic cloves, thinly sliced

2 cups dry white wine, preferably a dry Riesling

1 bay leaf

4 juniper berries

2 thyme sprigs

4 black peppercorns

2 thick slices smoked ham, each about
  7 ounces

2 tablespoons vegetable oil

4 good-quality link sausages

4 bone-in fresh or smoked pork chops,
  each about 7 ounces

1 pound Yukon Gold potatoes, peeled

1 large handful flat-leaf parsley leaves,
  chopped

SERVES 4 (generously) | **PREPARATION TIME** 15 minutes | **COOKING TIME** 2½ hours

CHOUCROUTE GARNI

Choucroute garni can only be described as a pork feast with cabbage—it's certainly a hearty dish! It can be made with any combination of fresh and salted pork, so I have used widely available cuts, but feel free to make your own meaty substitutions.

1] Preheat the oven to 325°F. Rinse the sauerkraut under cold running water, then leave to drain in a colander.

2] Put the butter in a large Dutch oven or a heavy-bottomed saucepan with an ovenproof handle and lid over low heat. When the butter is melted, add the onion and garlic and cook 8 to 10 minutes, stirring occasionally, until soft. Add the sauerkraut, wine, bay leaf, juniper berries, thyme and peppercorns, then turn up the heat and bring to a boil.

3] Nestle the smoked ham in the sauerkraut mixture and cover the casserole, then transfer it to the oven and cook 1½ hours. Toward the end of the cooking time, heat the oil in a large skillet, add the sausages and chops and cook until brown, turning them occasionally. Don't overcrowd the skillet—you will probably have to cook them in two batches.

4] Remove the casserole from the oven and check there is still a little liquid left. If it is very dry, then add a splash of water or extra wine. Sit the sausages and chops on top of the sauerkraut, re-cover the casserole and return to the oven 30 minutes.

5] Meanwhile, put the potatoes in a large saucepan of salted water over high heat. Bring to a boil, then turn the heat down and simmer 20 minutes until tender.

6] Cut each piece of ham in half to make four portions. Pick out and remove the bay leaf, juniper berries, thyme and peppercorns from the sauerkraut. Serve the choucroute garni with the potatoes. Scatter the parsley over the top before serving.

1¼ cups dry navy beans

1 tablespoon duck or goose fat or vegetable oil

4 duck legs

4 Toulouse sausages

3½ ounces lardons, cubetti di pancetta or diced thick smoked bacon

1 onion, finely chopped

1 carrot, diced

1 celery stalk, diced

4 garlic cloves, peeled

½ cup dry white wine

1 can (15-oz.) crushed tomatoes

2 thyme sprigs

1 bay leaf

salt and freshly ground black pepper

crisp green salad, to serve

SERVES 4 | **PREPARATION TIME** 30 minutes, plus overnight soaking | **COOKING TIME** 3¼ hours

CASSOULET

A beautiful marriage of flavors, textures and different types of meat. This is a truly wonderful dish that deserves its place at any great dinner table.

1] Put the haricot beans in a large bowl and cover with plenty of cold water. Leave to soak overnight. Drain the beans, transfer them to a large saucepan and cover with plenty of fresh water. Put the saucepan over high heat. Bring to a boil and boil the beans briskly 10 minutes. Drain the beans and leave to one side.

2] Put the duck fat in a large Dutch oven or a heavy-bottomed saucepan with ovenproof handle and lid over medium heat. Add the duck legs, skin-side down, and brown 5 to 6 minutes until the skin is golden. Turn the legs over and brown the flesh side, then transfer to a plate. Add the sausages and brown all over, then transfer to the plate.

3] Add the lardons, onion, carrot and celery to the casserole and cook 6 to 8 minutes, stirring occasionally, until the vegetables are soft. Add the beans, garlic, wine, tomatoes, thyme and bay leaf. Season with black pepper, but do not add any salt at this stage, because it will toughen the beans. Fill the tomato can with water and add to the casserole. Bring to a boil over high heat, then turn down the heat, cover and simmer 30 minutes. Meanwhile, preheat the oven to 325°F.

4] Nestle the duck legs and sausages into the beans. Re-cover the casserole, place in the oven and bake 2 hours until the beans are tender. Check the pan after 1 hour, and add a little extra water if the beans looks dry.

5] Just before serving, remove the duck legs and sausages from the pan. Pull the duck meat away from the bones in large chunks and slice the sausages thickly. Season the beans with salt and pepper, remove the bay leaf and thyme and mash the garlic cloves into the sauce. Serve the beans topped with the duck and sausages, and with a crisp green salad by the side.

HOW TO BRAISE A PORK ROAST

Braise comes from the French word *braiser*—a tightly covered pot that sits over hot coals—although it has now become a universal culinary term for cooking meat and vegetables slowly in a covered container with a small amount of liquid.

The combination of low temperature, moist heat and long cooking time makes braising ideal for tougher cuts of meat and particularly ones that lack a good marbling of fat, such as pork leg or hog jowl. Having said that, fattier cuts like shoulder or Boson butt braise well, too. You can also braise more tender cuts, such as tenderloin or loin, but as these are usually cooked for only a short period of time, they can be difficult to time accurately.

During the braising process the meat transforms itself from tough and chewy to soft and tender. The large piece of meat (you can also braise smaller pieces) is automatically basted while it cooks, because the steam from the cooking liquid hits the lid of the pot and then runs down onto the meat. As an added bonus, the connective tissues melt as gelatin into the cooking liquid, leaving an enriched sauce to serve with the meat.

The Dutch oven or roasting pan for braising should be fairly thick and heavy so the heat is kept constant during cooking, and the lid or foil cover needs to fit tightly to prevent any of the liquid evaporating. Braising can be done on the stovetop over very low heat, or in the oven at a low temperature; either way there are five steps to follow. The first is to brown the meat. This both adds color to the meat and creates a *fond*, which comes from the browning of the meat and any caramelized juices sticking to the bottom of the pan, adding richness to the finished dish. To brown the meat, pat it dry and season it well with salt and pepper, then add a little oil to the Dutch oven to help the process along. The meat should be browned over medium heat—too low and the meat will just steam, but too high and the bottom of the pan will start to burn, giving a bitter flavor to the finished dish.

The second stage is to add aromatics, such as garlic, herbs and vegetables. Onions, carrots and celery are common, but other robust vegetables like fennel and parsnips can also be used. As the cooking time is long, the vegetables should be left in fairly large pieces.

The next step is to add liquid, and because not much is added it should be flavorful. Wine is a popular choice, although good-quality stock is also great. Add the liquid to the casserole and let it bubble, stirring with a wooden spoon to start to release the *fond* or caramelized bits on the bottom and side of the pot. Always use a tight-fitting lid so the meat can cook slowly in the oven or on the stovetop as long as is necessary to become tender.

The next stage, after cooking, is to let the braised joint rest for a short time off the heat. This lets the fibers in the meat relax, making it easier to cut. The final stage is finishing the sauce, which might need reducing by boiling or thickening with a flour and butter paste, or it might need extra liquid, depending on the recipe.

"SHOW ME HOW" TO BRAISE THE PORK ROAST

4½ pounds bone-in shoulder or Boston butt
roast, or 2¾ pounds boneless shoulder
or Boston butt roast, skin and most of the
fat removed

1 tablespoon olive oil

1 large onion, thickly sliced

2 garlic cloves, bruised

1 large carrot, thickly sliced

1 celery stalk, thickly sliced

2 rosemary sprigs

finely grated zest and juice from 1 large orange

1 cup vegetable stock

1¼ cups fruity red wine

2 teaspoons butter, soft

2 teaspoons all-purpose flour

salt and freshly ground black pepper

SERVES 4 to 6 | **PREPARATION TIME** 20 minutes | **COOKING TIME** 4½ hours

RED WINE & ORANGE BRAISED PORK SHOULDER [*pictured overleaf*]

1] Preheat the oven to 325°F. Season the pork all over with salt and pepper.

2] Put the oil in a large Dutch oven or a heavy-bottomed roasting pan over medium heat. Brown the pork 2 to 3 minutes on each side until colored all over, then remove from the casserole. Add the onion, garlic, carrot and celery and cook 2 to 3 minutes. Return the pork to the casserole and add the rosemary and orange zest and juice. Pour in the stock and wine.

3] Return the pork to the casserole, then turn off the heat and cover tightly with a lid (or a double layer of foil, if using a roasting pan). Transfer the casserole to the oven and cook about 4 hours or until the pork is very tender and falling away from the bone.

4] Remove the pork from the casserole and transfer to a warm plate. Cover with foil and leave in a warm place while you make the sauce. Skim the fat from the surface of the cooking liquid, then strain it into a saucepan, pressing down on the vegetables in the strainer to extract as much liquid as possible. Put the saucepan over high heat and boil the liquid until it reduces by two-thirds; this will take 8 to 10 minutes, depending on the size of your pan. Meanwhile, mix together the butter and flour to make a smooth paste.

5] Turn down the heat to low and whisk the flour mixture into the sauce, a little at a time. Simmer the sauce 2 minutes until it thickens slightly. Season with salt and pepper.

6] Remove the pork from the bone in large chunks and serve with the sauce spooned over.

JOHNNIE'S TIP

For cracklings, try to keep the fat attached to the skin when removing it. Score the skin with a sharp knife at ⅛-inch intervals and put it on a baking sheet. Sprinkle with coarse kosher or sea salt and roast for the last hour of the pork's cooking time.

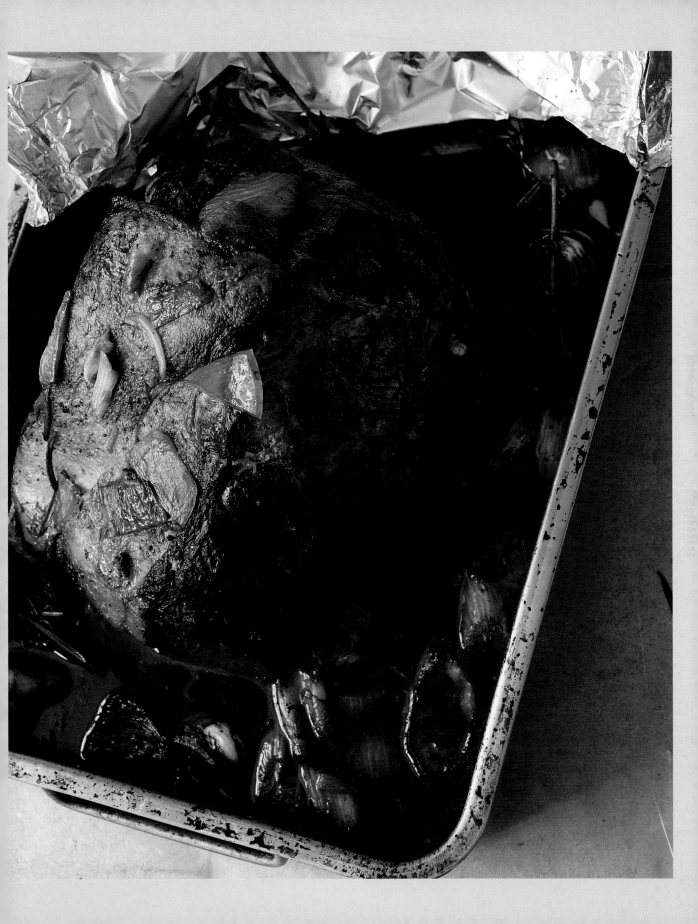

1 tablespoon vegetable oil

8 hog jowls

2 large fennel bulbs, stems trimmed and fronds reserved

1 onion, sliced

1 carrot, sliced

1 cup red wine

1 cup vegetable stock

2 thyme sprigs

1 bay leaf

1 star anise

4 teaspoons unsalted butter, soft

2 tablespoons dry white vermouth

1 teaspoon all-purpose flour

salt and freshly ground black pepper

1 recipe quantity Johnnie's Mashed Potatoes (see page 215), to serve

SERVES 4 | **PREPARATION TIME** 20 minutes | **COOKING TIME** 2¼ hours

HOG JOWLS WITH CARAMELIZED FENNEL

1] Put the oil in a large Dutch oven or a heavy-bottomed saucepan over medium heat. Season the jowls. When the oil is shimmering, brown the jowls 5 minutes on each side, then transfer to a plate. You might have to cook the jowls in batches.

2] Put the stems of each fennel bulb in the pan with the onion and carrot and cook 5 to 6 minutes until soft slightly. Pour in the wine and stock and add the thyme, bay leaf and star anise. Nestle the hog jowls into the vegetables and add a little water, if needed, to cover them partially. Bring to a boil, then turn down the heat to very low, cover and simmer 1½ to 2 hours until the jowls are very tender.

3] Toward the end of the cooking time, cut each fennel bulb into 6 pieces vertically. Melt 3 teaspoons of the butter in a large skillet over medium heat. When foaming, add the fennel, vermouth and 2 tablespoons water. Bring to a boil, then turn down the heat to low, cover and cook 8 minutes, turning the fennel over after 4 minutes. Uncover the pan, turn up the heat to high and cook 2 to 3 minutes longer until the liquid evaporates and the underside of the fennel is slightly caramelized. Flip the fennel over and cook 1 minute longer, then remove from the heat and keep warm.

4] Remove the jowls from the casserole and keep warm. Strain the cooking liquid, then discard the thyme, bay leaf and star anise and reserve the vegetables. Return the liquid to the casserole and boil until reduced by about one-third—you need about 1 cup. Return the reserved vegetables to the sauce to warm through.

5] Mix the remaining butter with the flour to make a smooth paste, then whisk it into the sauce, a little at a time. Bring the sauce back to a boil, whisking, then turn down the heat and simmer 1 minute until it thickens. Serve the jowls on top of the caramelized fennel. Spoon the sauce and vegetables over and sprinkle with the reserved fennel fronds. Serve with the mashed potatoes.

1½ teaspoons salt

1½ teaspoons fennel seeds

2 fresh pork knuckles, each about 3¾ pounds

2 tablespoons vegetable oil

2 onions, thinly sliced

1 cup dry hard cider, or ½ cup apple juice mixed with ½ cup water

⅛ teaspoon freshly ground black pepper

1 recipe quantity Johnnie's Mashed Potatoes (see page 215) and Wilted Spinach (see page 218), to serve

SERVES 4 to 6 | **PREPARATION TIME** 20 minutes | **COOKING TIME** 2½ hours

BRAISED PORK KNUCKLE IN CIDER

Pork knuckle, or pork tip, is most often eaten cured as a ham hock, rather than fresh, but this economical cut is perfect for roasting or braising. You might need to order it in advance from a butcher, and, if you do, request knuckles from the rear legs, because they are meatier than those from the front legs.

1] Preheat the oven to 325°F. Grind the salt and fennel seeds together using a mini food processor or mortar and pestle, then mix in plenty of black pepper.

2] Put the pork knuckles on a large cutting board and score the skin at ½-inch intervals. Rub the fennel mixture all over the knuckles, making sure plenty gets into the cuts in the skin.

3] Put the oil in a large roasting pan over high heat. When the oil is shimmering, sear the knuckles, one at a time, until brown all over. Take the pan off the heat, sit the knuckles flesh-side-down in the pan and add the onions and cider. Cover the pan with a double layer of foil, sealing it tightly and cook 1 hour. Turn the pan around and cook 1 hour longer until the pork can be pulled away easily from the bones. Remove the pan from the oven and increase the temperature to 425°F.

4] Transfer the pork knuckles to a baking sheet and return to the oven 30 minutes to crisp the skin. Meanwhile, bring the juices in the roasting pan to a boil and boil until they reduce by half. You might need to add a little water to the pan—there should be about 1¾ cups gravy. Season the gravy with salt and pepper and transfer to a warm gravy boat.

5] Put the pork knuckles on a serving platter and cut the skin and flesh into large chunks. Serve with the gravy, mashed potatoes and wilted spinach.

2 large smoked ham hocks, each about
   2¼ pounds
3 cups dry hard cider, or 1½ cups apple juice
   mixed with 1½ cups water
1 onion, halved
1 carrot, scrubbed and halved
1 celery stalk, halved
6 black peppercorns
1 star anise
1 bay leaf
2 thyme sprigs
2 tablespoons honey

LEEK CHAMP

5 cups peeled Yukon Gold potatoes, cut into
   1¼-inch cubes
3 tablespoons unsalted butter
3 leeks, trimmed and thinly sliced
4 scallions, thinly sliced
4 tablespoons heavy cream
salt and freshly ground black pepper

SERVES 4 | **PREPARATION TIME** 30 minutes | **COOKING TIME** 3¼ hours

BRAISED HAM HOCK WITH LEEK CHAMP [*pictured overleaf*]

1] Put the ham hocks in a large, heavy-bottomed saucepan. Pour in the cider and top up with enough cold water just to cover the hocks. Add the onion, carrot, celery, peppercorns, star anise, bay leaf and thyme, then bring to a boil over high heat. Skim away any scum that rises to the surface, then turn down the heat to low, cover and simmer 2 to 2½ hours until the meat starts to fall away from the bones.

2] Preheat the oven to 400°F. Remove the hocks from the saucepan and transfer them to a medium-sized roasting pan. Remove the skin from the hocks and discard. Scoop scant 1 cup of the cooking liquid into a measuring jug and whisk in the honey. Pour this over the hocks, put the roasting pan in the oven and roast the hocks 40 minutes, basting them with the liquid in the pan every 10 minutes.

3] Meanwhile to make the leek champ, cook the potatoes in a large saucepan of boiling salted water 15 to 20 minutes until tender. Drain the potatoes and leave in the colander 10 minutes to steam dry. Return the potatoes to the saucepan and mash thoroughly.

4] Melt the butter in a large skillet over medium heat. When foaming, add the leeks and cook 10 to 15 minutes, stirring occasionally, until very soft. Add the scallions and cook 2 minutes longer, then stir in the cream and remove from the heat. Put the potatoes over low heat and stir in the leek mixture a little at a time, then season to taste.

5] Pull the meat away from the ham hocks in large chunks. Serve with the champ.

JOHNNIE'S TIP

Ham hocks can sometimes be very salty and the best way to test this is to fry a small slither of the uncooked ham in a little oil. If it is too salty, simmer the hocks in a pan of water 10 minutes. Drain the hocks and return to the pan, then add the cider and continue with the recipe.

3 pounds 5 ounces smoked, cured, uncooked ham roast

1 onion, halved

1 carrot, halved

1 celery stalk

4-inch piece gingerroot, cut into ½-inch slices (no need to peel)

6 black peppercorns

2 tablespoons Dijon mustard

2 teaspoons ground ginger

about 15 whole cloves

3 tablespoons turbinado sugar

1 recipe quantity of Creamy Garlic Potatoes (see page 216)

SERVES 4 (with leftovers) | **PREPARATION TIME** 20 minutes, plus rinsing, soaking and resting | **COOKING TIME** 2 hours

HOMECOOKED HAM IN GINGER & MUSTARD GLAZE

If you prefer to use a bone-in ham, reduce the simmering time to 50 minutes per 2¼ pounds, or 25 minutes per pound. The baking time remains the same. If you can only find a fully-cooked ham, reheat it following the supplier's directions. Increase the oven temperature to 425°F and glaze the ham as in the recipe.

1] Rinse and soak the ham according to the supplier's instructions. Put the ham in a large saucepan and cover with water. Add the onion, carrot, celery, gingerroot and peppercorns and bring to a boil. Skim away any foamy scum that rises to the surface, then turn down the heat to low, cover and simmer 1½ hours. (If your ham is larger in size, calculate the cooking time as 1 hour per 2¼ pounds or 30 minutes per pound.) Make sure the liquid in the pan does not boil madly—the bubbles should just gently rise to the surface. Transfer the ham to a cutting board and let it cool slightly.

2] Preheat the oven to 425°F. Line a baking sheet with foil. Using a sharp knife, cut the skin away from the ham, leaving a thin layer of fat. Score a diamond pattern in the fat, taking care not to cut into the meat. Mix together the mustard and ground ginger and spread it over the surface of the fat, then stud every other corner of the diamond pattern with a clove. Sprinkle the sugar over the mustard.

3] Bake the ham 20 minutes, turning the pan halfway through, until the glaze is sticky and tangy. Leave the ham to rest 30 minutes before slicing and serving with the creamy garlic potatoes. Alternatively, leave to cool completely and refrigerate before serving.

JOHNNIE'S TIP

Nowadays, most hams have a fairly mild cure so should not be too salty. If you are not sure, however, cut a little piece from the uncooked ham and fry it in a little vegetable oil before tasting. If it is too salty, soak the ham in cold water 12 hours, changing the water after 6 hours. Drain and rinse, then continue with the recipe above.

"SHOW ME HOW" TO COOK AND GLAZE THE HAM

ACCOMPANIMENTS

Vegetables and potatoes might be regarded as a supporting act, but a good meal is always bolstered by something special on the side. Plain greens have a certain Puritan appeal, but add a little bacon and cream, or garlic and almonds, or maybe a little gingerroot and soy and they are transformed from a necessity into a delight. Sticky Red Cabbage is as tempting as it sounds, and you would need an iron will not to succumb to the golden and crisp Goose Fat Roast Potatoes or smooth and buttery Johnnie's Mashed Potatoes. You can't beat a classic Applesauce with pork, and this one is made with baked apples. This firm favorite is also given a new twist as a delicious caramelized Apple Jam. Don't think of these as just "extras"—they are stars in their own right!

TOMATO PUREE

MAKES 6 cups | PREPARATION TIME 15 minutes | COOKING TIME 1 hour 10 minutes

4 tablespoons olive oil • 2 large onions, finely chopped • 2 celery stalks, finely diced • 1 carrot, finely diced • 4 garlic cloves, crushed • 6 cans (15-oz.) crushed tomatoes • 1 tablespoon sugar • 4 good-quality black olives in oil, drained • 2 large bay leaves • salt and pepper (optional)

1] Put the oil in a large saucepan over very low heat. Add the onions, celery, carrot and garlic and cook very gently 20 to 30 minutes, stirring regularly. The vegetables should be very soft and sweet and look slightly sticky.

2] Add the remaining ingredients and bring to a boil, then turn down the heat and simmer 40 minutes until the sauce thickens slightly. Remove the olives and bay leaves and leave the sauce to cool slightly, then blend until smooth.

3] I tend not to season the tomato puree at this stage, because it will be seasoned when used in other recipes. If you want to serve it as an accompaniment, however, season with salt and pepper. Use the puree as needed or leave to cool and then freeze in useful portions in resealable containers.

CREAMY GRAVY

SERVES 4 | PREPARATION TIME 5 minutes | COOKING TIME 10 minutes

2 teaspoons unsalted butter • 2 teaspoons all-purpose flour • 4 tablespoons dry white wine or extra chicken stock • 1 cup chicken stock • 1 tablespoon heavy cream • salt and freshly ground black pepper

1] Melt the butter in a small saucepan over medium heat, then add the flour, stirring constantly. Stir 2 minutes to cook out the raw flavor. Add the wine, if using, and whisk until combined.

2] Add the stock, a little at a time, whisking constantly. Bring to a boil, then turn down the heat and simmer until the gravy reduces and thickens slightly. Add the cream, stir and heat through gently. Season to taste, then pour into a warm gravy boat just before serving.

APPLE JAM

SERVES 4 to 6 | **PREPARATION TIME** 10 minutes | **COOKING TIME** 15 minutes

2 tablespoons chilled unsalted butter, thinly sliced • ½ cup sugar • 2 large green apples, such as Granny Smiths, about 12 ounces total weight, peeled, quartered, cored and diced • 1 teaspoon lemon juice • ½ vanilla bean

1] Lay the slices of butter over the bottom of a large, nonstick skillet. Sprinkle the sugar over the butter in an even layer. Put the pan over low heat and let the butter and sugar melt together until there is not any graininess left in the sugar. If you have difficulty getting the sugar to melt completely, swirl 1 tablespoon water into the mixture and continue to heat gently until the sugar dissolves.

2] Increase the heat to high and bring the sugar mixture to a boil. Let the mixture boil until it turns a deep amber color; this should take 6 to 8 minutes. You should not stir the mixture, but you can swirl the pan once or twice if the outside edge is darkening too quickly.

3] Take the pan off the heat and add the apple pieces (take care, because the caramel might spit a little), then stir in the lemon juice. Return the pan to the heat and bring back to a boil, then boil 2 minutes until the syrup thickens slightly again. Take the pan off the heat and leave to cool—the jam thickens as it cools. Scrape the seeds from the vanilla bean and stir these into the jam.

4] The apple jam will keep in the refrigerator 3 to 4 days in an airtight container. Bring to room temperature or warm slightly before serving.

APPLESAUCE

SERVES 4 | **PREPARATION TIME** 10 minutes | **COOKING TIME** 30 to 60 minutes

1 pound 2 ounces eating apples, such as Spartan, cored • 1 to 2 tablespoons sugar, to taste • 1 to 2 teaspoons lemon juice, to taste

1] Preheat the oven to 325°F.

2] Run a sharp knife around the equator of each apple to score the skin. Put the apples on a baking sheet and bake until soft; this will take 30 to 60 minutes depending on the size and variety of apple you use.

3] Let the apples cool slightly, then pull or cut them in half and scoop out the flesh, discarding the skins. Blend the flesh using a hand blender or an upright blender until smooth. Stir in the sugar and lemon juice, to taste. You are looking for a good balance of sweetness and tartness.

4] The applesauce will keep in the refrigerator up to 3 days in an airtight container. Bring to room temperature before serving.

GNOCCHI

SERVES 4 | **PREPARATION TIME** 1 hour, chilling | **COOKING TIME** 50 minutes

2 potatoes, such as Yukon Gold, unpeeled, about 1 pound 2 ounces total weight • 1 egg yolk
• ½ teaspoon salt • 1²/₃ cups Italian OO flour, plus extra for dusting

1] Put the unpeeled potatoes into a large saucepan of cold salted water. Bring to a boil over high heat, then turn down the heat and simmer 30 to 40 minutes, part-covered, until tender and a table knife can be easily inserted into the middle of each potato. Drain the potatoes and leave them to cool slightly—they should be cool enough to handle but still warm.

2] Peel the potatoes and transfer them to a large bowl. Mash them very well—there should not be any lumps, because these will be very noticeable in the finished gnocchi. If you have a potato ricer or a food mill, pass the potatoes through either for a perfect, lump-free texture.

3] Make a well in the middle of the mashed potatoes and add the egg yolk and salt, plus three-quarters of the flour. Gently mix everything together, adding more flour as needed to make a smooth and firm but still flexible dough.

4] Line two baking sheets with waxed paper and dust them generously with flour.

5] Take one-quarter of the dough and place on a lightly floured work surface. Loosely cover the remaining dough with a piece of plastic wrap. Roll out the piece of dough into a long rope, about ¼ inch thick. As you roll, spread your fingers out to help the dough stretch into a rope. If it becomes too long for you to handle, cut the rope in half and work with one piece at a time.

6] Cut the rope into sections about 1 inch long with a flour-dusted knife. Dip the tines of a fork into some flour, then take one of the pieces of cut dough and roll it over the back of the fork so it becomes ridged. Repeat with the remaining dough.

7] Transfer the gnocchi to the prepared baking sheets, dusting the finished gnocchi with a little extra flour. Once all of the gnocchi have been made, loosely cover with plastic wrap and store in the refrigerator 1 hour. The gnocchi can also be frozen at this stage on the baking sheets. Transfer them to a resealable bag once they are firm and cook direct from frozen.

8] To cook the gnocchi, bring a large saucepan of salted water to a boil. The cooking time can vary depending on the exact size of the gnocchi, so it is a good idea to cook one or two as testers to see how long they take. Although recipes often say that the gnocchi will float to the surface of the water when ready, this is not always the case and it is easier to test a couple first; they are cooked when they no longer have a raw floury taste. This type of gnocchi usually takes about 4 minutes to cook, and 4½ to 5 minutes if cooking from frozen. You might need to cook them in batches.

9] Add the gnocchi to the pan of water and return the water to a boil, then lower the heat and simmer 4 minutes until cooked. Don't let the water boil too hard, because if this happens the gnocchi will break up. Using a slotted spoon or small strainer, scoop the gnocchi out of the water (don't drain them into a colander or strainer, because they will break up). Blot any excess water from the bottom of the spoon with paper towels before transferring the gnocchi to their sauce, or serving as liked.

CHUNKY FRIES

SERVES 4 | **PREPARATION TIME** 20 minutes | **COOKING TIME** 25 minutes

4 large potatoes, such as Yukon Gold, about 2 pounds 12 ounces total weight, peeled and ends cut to make a flat surface • vegetable oil, for deep-frying • kosher or sea salt flakes

1] Stand one of the potatoes up on its flat end and cut down the sides so you have a rough rectangular shape; repeat with the remaining potatoes. The trimmings can either be discarded or covered with water and kept in the refrigerator up to 2 days and used for making mashed potatoes.

2] Cut each potato into fat, rectangular fries, each around ¾ inch thick. Put the potatoes in a large saucepan of cold salted water over high heat. Bring the water to a boil, then turn down the heat and simmer 8 minutes until the potatoes are just tender.

3] Carefully drain the potatoes, then transfer them to a wire rack so they steam dry. Pour enough oil into a large saucepan or deep-fat fryer to fill by one-third. Heat the oil to 375°F. Line a baking sheet with a double layer of paper towels.

4] Preheat the oven to 200°F. Carefully lower half of the potatoes into the hot oil and fry 6 to 8 minutes until golden. Don't overcrowd the pan and make sure you reheat the oil to 375°F between batches. Transfer the fries to the prepared baking sheet to drain, and keep warm in the oven while you cook the remainder. Sprinkle with kosher salt before serving.

JOHNNIE'S MASHED POTATOES

SERVES 4 to 6 | **PREPARATION TIME** 25 minutes | **COOKING TIME** 45 minutes

1 pound 10 ounces floury potatoes, peeled and cut into 2-inch chunks • 5 tablespoons unsalted butter • ⅓ cup heavy cream • salt and ground white pepper

1] Put the potatoes into a large saucepan of cold salted water over high heat.

2] Bring the water to a boil, then turn down the heat to low. Skim away any foam that comes to the surface and let the potatoes cook very gently 35 to 40 minutes until a table knife can be easily inserted into the potatoes. The water in the saucepan should just have a few bubbles rising to the surface and should not boil.

3] Drain the potatoes and spread them out on a baking sheet. Let them steam dry 10 minutes, turning them over halfway through. Meanwhile, put the butter and cream in a small saucepan over low heat and warm until the butter melts.

4] While the potatoes are still warm, mash them in a clean saucepan until there are not any lumps. Use a potato ricer or food mill if you have one to guarantee a smooth, lump-free texture.

5] Put the saucepan over very low heat. Using a spatula, fold in the warm cream and butter mixture a little at a time until it is all incorporated. Season with salt and a little white pepper and serve immediately.

GOOSE FAT ROAST POTATOES

SERVES 4 to 6 | **PREPARATION TIME** 10 minutes | **COOKING TIME** 1¼ hours

2¼ pounds Yukon Gold potatoes, peeled and halved or quartered, depending on their size
• ½ cup goose fat • 4 garlic cloves, bruised • kosher or sea salt

1] Preheat the oven to 400°F.
2] Put the potatoes in a large saucepan of cold salted water over high heat. Bring the water to a boil, then turn down the heat to low. Skim away any foam from the surface of the water and let the potatoes simmer about 20 minutes until a table knife can be inserted easily. Keep an eye on them, because you want the outside of the potatoes to be soft so the surface is textured, but not so cooked they break up.
3] Drain the potatoes and let them stand in a colander 10 minutes to steam dry, shaking them slightly halfway through to make sure the ones on the bottom also dry out. Give the potatoes a good shake in the colander so the outsides become rough and slightly fluffy; this guarantees a crisp surface after roasting.
4] Meanwhile, divide the goose fat between 2 baking sheets that are at least ¼ inch deep. Add 2 of the garlic cloves to each baking tray and put them in the oven to heat the fat and to infuse it slightly with the garlic flavor.
5] Remove one baking sheet from the oven and carefully remove and discard the garlic. Arrange half the potatoes on the baking sheet, turning each one in the hot oil until evenly coated, then return the baking sheet to the oven. Repeat with the second baking sheet and remaining potatoes.
6] Roast 15 minutes, then take the baking sheets out of the oven and turn the potatoes. Return them to the oven, switching the baking trays and turning them around. Roast 30 minutes longer, turning the potatoes every 10 minutes and rotating the baking sheets so the potatoes become evenly golden and crisp. Transfer the roast potatoes to a tray lined with a double layer of paper towels and blot briefly before sprinkling with kosher salt. Serve immediately.

CREAMY GARLIC POTATOES

SERVES 4 to 6 | **PREPARATION TIME** 20 minutes | **COOKING TIME** 45 minutes

softened unsalted butter, for greasing • 1¼ cups heavy cream • 1¼ cups whole milk • 4 garlic cloves,
peeled and thinly sliced • 2 pounds white potatoes, such as Yukon Gold • leaves from 2 thyme sprigs • salt
and freshly ground black pepper

1] Preheat the oven to 400°F. Generously grease a small roasting pan or baking dish with the butter.
2] Put the cream, milk and garlic into a large saucepan. Peel the potatoes and slice them as thinly as possible into circles—a mandolin makes easy work of this. Add the potatoes to the pan as you cut them. Push the slices under the liquid to prevent them turning brown. Add the thyme leaves and season with salt and pepper.
3] Put the saucepan over medium heat and bring the liquid up to a boil. Turn down the heat to low and simmer the potatoes 5 minutes. Remove the pan from the heat and, using a slotted spoon, carefully transfer the potatoes to the buttered pan. Make sure the potato slices are pushed well into the corners of the dish. Spoon enough of the cream mixture over to just cover the potatoes.

4] Bake about 30 minutes until the top is golden brown. The exact timing depends on the thickness of the slices, but the potatoes are ready when most of the liquid is absorbed and they are tender if you test them with the tip of a table knife. Remove the roasting pan from the oven and let the potatoes stand 10 minutes before serving.

5] If you want to make the potatoes in advance, line the pan with parchment paper, with the paper coming above two sides of the pan to act as "handles." Grease the paper with butter. Prepare and cook the potatoes as in Steps 2 through 4 and, once cooked, let them cool, then refrigerate them up to 2 days. When fully chilled and firm, use the paper "handles" to lift the potatoes out of the pan in one piece onto a cutting board. Cut the potatoes into portions and transfer to a baking sheet lined with parchment paper. Reheat in an oven preheated to 350°F about 20 minutes until warmed through.

BUTTERED RICE

SERVES 4 | PREPARATION TIME 25 minutes | COOKING TIME 15 minutes

2 tablespoons unsalted butter • 1 cup basmati or jasmine rice • ½ teaspoon salt

1] Put the butter in a medium-sized saucepan over medium heat. When it melts, add the rice and let it cook in the butter 3 to 4 minutes, stirring constantly.

2] Add 2 cups water and the salt to the rice. Bring to a boil, then turn down the heat and simmer 7 to 8 minutes until the water is no longer visible above the top of the rice. Turn off the heat, cover the pan tightly with the lid and leave to stand 20 minutes. Fluff up the rice with a fork before serving.

VARIATION
For a spicy version, finely chop 1 small onion and fry it in the melted butter 7 to 8 minutes until soft, before adding 1 teaspoon mustard seeds along with the rice. Continue as in Step 1.

GINGER BOK CHOY

SERVES 4 | PREPARATION TIME 10 minutes | COOKING TIME 10 minutes

1 tablespoon sunflower or vegetable oil • 1-inch piece gingerroot, peeled and grated • 4 bok choy, halved • 1 teaspoon toasted sesame oil • 1 teaspoon soy sauce

1] Heat the oil in a large, nonstick skillet over high heat. Add the ginger and let it sizzle 30 seconds, then add the bok choy, cut-side down; the pan will look a bit crowded at first, but as the leaves wilt there will be enough room. Cook the bok choy 2 to 3 minutes until tinged with brown.

2] Turn the bok choy over and cook 2 minutes longer. Add ½ cup water to the pan with the sesame oil and soy sauce and bring to a boil. Turn down the heat and simmer 5 to 6 minutes, turning halfway, until the liquid almost evaporates and the bok choy is tender.

WILTED SPINACH

SERVES 4 | **PREPARATION TIME** 10 minutes | **COOKING TIME** 10 minutes

1 pound leaf spinach, tough stems removed, or 14 ounces baby spinach • 1 stick (½ cup) unsalted butter • salt and freshly ground black pepper

1] Fill a sink with cold water, add the spinach and swish it around in the water, then lift it into a colander. Drain the water and rinse away any grit, then fill the sink again and wash the spinach a second time. Let the spinach drain thoroughly or dry in a clean dish towel or use a salad spinner.

2] Put half of the butter in a large saucepan over medium heat. When the butter melts, add half the spinach and cook 2 to 3 minutes until it wilts. Constantly turn the spinach, using a pair of tongs or 2 wooden spoons, so it wilts evenly. Transfer the spinach to a strainer and let the excess liquid drain away. Repeat with the remaining butter and spinach. Return the cooked spinach to the pan and heat gently 1 to 2 minutes, then season with salt and pepper before serving.

VARIATIONS
• Add a large pinch of freshly grated nutmeg to the spinach with the salt and pepper in Step 2.
• For an Asian version, thinly slice 2 garlic cloves. Add half of the garlic to the butter when you cook the first batch of spinach, then repeat with the second batch. When you reheat the spinach, add a little grated gingerroot and sprinkle 2 teaspoons toasted sesame seeds over.

GREEN BEANS WITH GARLIC & ALMONDS

SERVES 4 | **PREPARATION TIME** 10 minutes | **COOKING TIME** 10 minutes

⅓ cup slivered almonds • 8 ounces green beans, trimmed • 3 tablespoons unsalted butter • 2 garlic cloves, crushed • salt and freshly ground black pepper

1] Put a large, nonstick skillet over medium-low heat. Add the almonds and toast 2 to 3 minutes until golden. Remove the pan from the heat, transfer the almonds to a plate and leave to one side.

2] Put a saucepan of cold salted water over high heat and bring to a boil. Add the beans, return the water to a boil and cook 2 to 3 minutes until the beans have lost their "squeakiness," but are still crisp. Drain the beans and immediately rinse them under cold running water until cold. Leave the beans to drain completely, or transfer to a clean dish towel and pat dry.

3] Melt the butter in the skillet over medium-high heat. Add the garlic and let it sizzle 10 seconds. Add the green beans and cook, stirring constantly, 2 to 3 minutes until heated through. Remove the pan from the heat, season with salt and pepper and serve with the toasted almonds scattered over the top.

STICKY RED CABBAGE

SERVES 4 | **PREPARATION TIME** 15 minutes, plus soaking | **COOKING TIME** 55 minutes

1 cup golden raisins • 1 stick (½ cup) unsalted butter • 5 cups very thinly sliced red cabbage
• ½ cup good-quality balsamic vinegar • ½ cup turbinado sugar • 1 cinnamon stick, about 3 inches long
• 2 star anise • salt and freshly ground black pepper

1] Put the golden raisins in a heatproof bowl and cover with water from a just-boiled kettle. Leave
to stand 30 minutes until soft, then drain.

2] Melt the butter in a large Dutch oven or a heavy-bottomed saucepan over medium heat. Add the
cabbage and turn it in the melted butter. Stir in the vinegar and sugar and 2 tablespoons water.

3] Tap the cinnamon stick with a rolling pin to crack it slightly, then add to the cabbage with the star
anise and drained golden raisins. Bring to a boil over high heat, then turn down the heat and simmer,
uncovered, about 50 minutes until the cabbage is soft and sticky. Give the cabbage an occasional
stir to stop it catching on the bottom of the pan.

4] Remove the cinnamon stick and star anise from the cabbage and season with salt and pepper
before serving.

SAVOY CABBAGE WITH LARDONS

SERVES 4 | **PREPARATION TIME** 10 minutes | **COOKING TIME** 15 minutes

5 cups thinly sliced Savoy cabbage • 3½ ounces lardons, chopped pancetta or diced thick
smoked bacon • 1 tablespoon butter • 2 tablespoons heavy cream • freshly ground black pepper

1] Put a large saucepan of cold salted water over high heat and bring to a boil. Add the cabbage and
return the water to a boil and boil 1 minute. Drain the cabbage and immediately rinse it under cold
running water until cold. Leave the cabbage to drain thoroughly or transfer it to a clean dish towel
and pat dry.

2] Put the lardons in a large, nonstick skillet or wok over low heat and fry 4 to 5 minutes until the fat
melts. Increase the heat to medium-high and fry the lardons 2 to 3 minutes until golden and crisp.

3] Add the butter to the skillet and let it melt, then add the cabbage and cream and cook 3 to 5 minutes,
stirring constantly, until the cabbage is heated through. Season with pepper (the lardons are very salty
so you probably won't need to add extra salt) and serve.

VARIATION
For a Christmas version, add scant 1 cup peeled and coarsely chopped cooked chestnuts to the pan
when you cook the cabbage in Step 3.

INDEX

ACKNOWLEDGMENTS

PUBLISHER'S NOTE

The Quick Response (QR) codes included throughout the book will link you to "How to'"videos, showing useful techniques to help you with the recipes. The QR codes work best on a smartphone or tablet with a camera resolution over 3MP. If you don't have access to a smartphone or tablet, or have any trouble using the QR codes, all the videos can be found at: www.ibiblios.co.uk/pig

AUTHOR'S ACKNOWLEDGMENTS

There are a handful of people I would like to thank in producing this book: Caroline Stearn, without whom this book and its contents would be nothing, Borra Garson (the gatekeeper @ DML), Grace Cheetham, Manisha Patel, Aya Nishimura and the beautiful photography from Yuki Sugiura......Thank you xxx

I'd also like to thank Lord March's Goodwood Home Farm, in Chichester, West Sussex, England, for supplying the most fantastic pork.

PICTURE ACKNOWLEDGMENTS

Pig illustration: Sailesh Patel
Page 6
Debbie Jones/Imaging Essence
Page 9
[1] Ernie Janes/NHPA
[2] John Eveson/FLPA
[3] Wayne Hutchinson/FLPA
[4] Chico Sanchez/Alamy
[5] Corbis Premium RF/Alamy
[6] INTERFOTO/Alamy
Page 224 (above)
Paul Miguel/FLPA